FOREWORD

This is a not your typical book ... e just 24 hours a day of which 6 ... you are sleeping. If you manage the hours you are awake wisely you can accomplish a lot! If you don't....time can be your enemy causing incredible stress on your mental health, your physical body and your emotional wellbeing. Poor time management causes a huge amount of stress. Shawn Chhabra has provided a fabulous resource with this book that can make you a time management expert....super fast!

Though it is an easy read it addresses and solves big problems that keep people from maximizing their achievement and peace of mind and even their health. Shawn gives simple, easy to understand advice that can be life changing! He has proven that time management and stress reduction go hand in hand.

This book is full of amazing, innovative insights and brilliant wisdom that impact lives, health, success and happiness. As a savvy businessman Shawn brings a wealth of experience, tools, stories and strategies to ensure that you do not keep running out of time or use it poorly causing unnecessary stress and major frustration.

With the wisdom in this book you will be able to master the waking hours in your life and live a more productive and happy life.

As an internationally recognized success expert I can say that Shawn has done a great job in explaining how to take control of your life by mastering the hours in your day! Carve out the time to read it right away. You will be glad you did!

Jack M. Zufelt
Mentor To Millions"
Author of the #1 best-selling book,
The DNA of Success, (now in 15 languages)

www.dnaofsuccess.com
Need a speaker for your next event?
www.jackzufeltspeaks.com

Praise

We've all heard that time is the one thing in life you can never get back. If you want to be "rich" in time, you've got to manage it very carefully, and it can be difficult to know where to start. Well, that's no longer difficult. Start RIGHT HERE with Shawn Chhabra's *Time Management.* You'll be glad you did!

-- Nick Nanton, Esq.
3-Time Emmy® Award Winning Director & Producer
Best-Selling Author
www.CelebrityBrandingAgency.com

Shawn Chhabra
Best Selling Author

Book Summary

Time management: *It's Time To Take Control of Your Time and Your Life and Learn How To Do That!*

Do you feel like you are not in control of your life? Do you struggle to figure out how to get everything done in a day? Are you worried that you can't stay organized or stay ahead of the game? If you want to take your life back and truly enjoy the time that you have, then the "Time Management" book is for you!

The "Time Management" is a book that shows you what it really means to stay in control of your life. Though you may feel bogged down by commitments and a lack of time to complete them all, sometimes it's simply a matter of staying organized. This book, written by Shawn Chhabra, can be an excellent tool in helping you to do just that.

It's Time To Take Control of Your Time and Your Life and Learn How To Do That

So many of us struggle with managing our commitments and understanding what our time is worth, and now it's time to get the answers. You will see through this book not only how to budget your time properly, but also how to prioritize each and every task so that you can manage your day accordingly. It doesn't matter what your specific time management issues are or how unorganized that you may feel, for this book can help you to pull it all together.

 If you want to be in control of your life and manage the various elements, this book can provide just the insight that you've been looking for. You will learn about helpful apps or new technology that can ensure you stay ahead of the game. Sometimes finding the right method of organizing your day and managing your tasks is all it takes.

You will see what you have likely been doing wrong, and how to turn that behavior around into a positive. You will learn some of the best time life management skills and how to truly get organized in your life. So if you are ready to make that change and move forward in a productive, healthy, and truly organized manner, this book will give you the courage to do so and to make truly positive changes in your life that really count.

The book will teach you how to avoid distractions and really focus on what you have to get done in a day. You will also learn the value of making a daily schedule for yourself so that it's all spelled out for you. Even if you have struggled in the past or given into the many distractions around you, this book will help you to turn those negatives into positives.

This Is How To Get To Positive Changes In Your Life
This book comes to you from author Shawn Chhabra who has shared his expertise in this area and others. He has provided organizational and life techniques through his series of books, and it shines through in this latest entry. This book offers his experience and knowledge, and you can mimic some of the positive habits that he has used in his businesses.

So if you are ready to make effective change in your life, this is how you get to that. Though you may struggle with time life management, you can take control once and for all. Seeing it all in black and white and really learning what you may have been doing wrong all along will help. Learning what the best and proper habits are to replace the wrong ones will ensure that you stay ahead of the game once and for all. The "Time Management" book will not only help you to get your time back, but it will also help you to improve your life along the way as well!

The "Time Management, Life Management, Stress Management" is a book that shows you what it really means to stay in control of your life. Though you may feel bogged down by commitments and a lack of time to complete them all, sometimes it's simply a matter of staying organized. Shawn Chhabra's Time Management book can be an excellent tool in helping you to do just that.

The book also includes additional material:

- BONUS CHAPTER: BY JACK M. ZUFELT
- Appendices Section: ADDITIONAL RESOURCES
- Appendix: Time Management Quotes
- Tips and Tricks for Handling the Stress and Time Management
- Breathing and Yoga Techniques for Stress Management (illustrated by Tameisha Shevelle Harrington)
- Appendix: Outsourcing Resources
- Appendix: Stress and Anxiety Reducer Healthy Food and Recipes

BONUS CHAPTER: BY JACK M. ZUFELT

This chapter is a very special gift Honorable Mr. Jack M. Zufelt

JACK ZUFELT is one of the most successful speakers and business consultants on the national and international scene.

Jack is a very popular keynote speaker. He conducts seminars and customized training programs as well as life-changing weekend retreats all over the world. His client list includes companies of all sizes including many Fortune 500 companies.

He is also the highest paid trainer in Network Marketing.

Jack's book, The DNA of Success, has catapulted him into the limelight as a celebrity business consultant, keynote speaker and trainer all around the world.

   Jack M. Zufelt
"Mentor to Millions"
Author of the #1 best-selling book,
The DNA of Success...Now in 15 Languages

Seen and heard on over 2,000 radio and TV talk shows including The TODAY SHOW and PBS

www.TheDNAofSuccessSystem.com

To book Jack to speak at your next event go to
www.jackzufeltspeaks.com
or call his office at: 303 741-9025

Jack M. Zufelt
"Mentor to Millions"

Table Of Content

Introduction

Why Your lack of Time Management Is Working Against You

Why You Need to Change Your Ways To Eliminate The Stress

Take Over—The Necessity of Managing Your Time

How Getting Organized Can Add More Time To Your Day

What Effective Time Management Can Add To Your Life

Outcomes of Poor Time Management

How Much Is Your Time Worth? (Define The Cost Of Your Time)

Avoiding Distractions and Focusing On What Really Matters—True Prioritization

Getting Back On Track After a Crazy or Offbeat Day

Technological Advances--Time Management Tools and Applications

Creating an Effective Daily Schedule That Works For You

Carving Out and Enjoying a Bit of Me Time

Keeping With Good Time Management Habits Moving Forward

Conclusion

BONUS CHAPTER: BY JACK M. ZUFELT

Appendices Section: ADDITIONAL RESOURCES
Appendix: Time Management Quotes
Tips and Tricks for Handling the Stress and Time Management
Breathing and Yoga Techniques for Stress Management (illustrated by **Tameisha Shevelle Harrington)**
Appendix: Outsourcing Resources
Appendix: Stress and Anxiety Reducer Healthy Food and Recipes

Dedication

I want to dedicate this book to Brian Tracy, a brilliant man
For whom I have the utmost respect and gratitude towards.
Brian is without a doubt one of the most inspirational and
motivational speakers in the world. His books and guidance
have taught me so very much!

I WANT TO GIVE A BIG THANK YOU TO....

My friend Mr. Nick Nanton, esquire, and his amazing management team, including J.W. and Lindsay Dicks who are geniuses! Mandy Tawbush was brilliant in guiding me through the complicated process. It is because of the efforts of these wonderful people that I have the prestigious opportunity of being a co-author with my mentor, Brian Tracy, in his book, The Winning Way!

I also want to give an extra special thanks to Mr. Jack M. Zufelt. a very amazing, internationally known, highly successful speaker, Best Selling Author and trainer, He gave me a lot of guidance, that really blessed me and….for contributing a bonus chapter for this book!

50% of the author's net proceeds from the book sale will be donated (in equal portions) to American Cancer Society *www.cancer.org* and Red Cross *www.redcross*.org

Copyright Notice

All rights reserved in accordance with the Copyrights, Designs and Patents Act 1988. No part of this book may be reproduced in any form or by any electronic or mechanical means including information storage and retrieval system without permission from the author(s) and publisher, except by a reviewer who may quote brief passages in a review. Any person who carries out any unauthorized act in relation to this publication may be liable to criminal prosecution and civil claims for damages.

Publisher: www.ShawnChhabra.com

Author: Shawn Chhabra

Illustrated by: Tameisha Shevelle Harrington

Legal Disclaimer

This book is not intended to treat, diagnose or prescribe. Author, Publishers, Editors, and all other contributors have provided this material for entirely educational purposes. Use(s) of this information is entirely the responsibility of those who choose to apply this information for their personal health and wellbeing. This information is not intended as prescription, prognosis or diagnosis for any disease or illness, and should not be used as a replacement for any medical treatment you may currently be undergoing. It is not intended to substitute the medical expertise and advice of your primary health care provider. We encourage you to discuss any decisions about treatment or care with your health care provider.

The mention of any product, service, or therapy is not an endorsement by the publisher and its affiliates. The information provided is solely the opinion of the individual(s) and is, again, for educational purposes only. Application of information provided without supervision of a licensed medical doctor is done so at the individuals own risk.

Introduction

The purpose of time management and getting more done in less time is to enable you to spend more face time with the people you care about and doing the things that give you the greatest amount of joy in life.
-- Brian Tracy

Sometimes it may seem that there isn't enough time to do everything that you need to. It's necessary that you develop efficient ways for managing your time to balance the demands of your daily life such as working, planning a vacation and making time for your family and friends. Over time, this can cause stress and fatigue, thus, affecting your ability on how to deal with your daily routines.

Struggling to figure out how to balance everything and how to work through the stress of everyday life is quite common. You are not alone in your desire to get control of your life back.

Having the intuition to notice that something is amiss is the first and most important step. Then taking action and working towards a solution is another way to move towards a productive future. This can all add up to not only managing your time better, but also working towards a balanced and healthier lifestyle in the process.

Time Management skills are very important in your everyday life, but also in many other aspects of life: from studying for examinations to working your way to the top of your career.

Once you have identified ways in which you can improve the management of your time, you can begin to adjust your routines and patterns of behavior to reduce any time-related stress in your life.

This book can help you defeat the scrambles of your everyday tasks by keeping your schedules organized, tasks on point and life intact.

Why Your Lack of Time Management Is Working Against You

Do you feel stressed each and every day? Do you often feel as though you can't possibly get everything done? Are you worried or anxious often? If some of these common signs sound familiar to you, then this is how a lack of time management can start to get to you after awhile. Not only can it work against your ability to concentrate and be productive, but it can also create a negative impact to your health as well.

If you feel as though you are working hard but never getting anything done, then it's time to take notice of that. When your lack of time management and organization is creating a negative impact in your life, it can often feel as though you are running in place and not getting anywhere. Does this sound familiar? You've dealt with this heavy weight on your life for long enough, now it's time to make positive changes.

Not Effectively Managing Your Time Can Hurt You In Many Ways

Though you probably don't realize it as you are deeply ingrained in the daily activities, all of the stress and strain each day is taking a toll on you. There is a very direct connection between poor time management and health problems, but we don't notice this until it's too late. If you keep at this pace and you keep running in place, it's going to cause bigger problems in your life than what you are experiencing now.

This isn't meant to scare you per se, but rather to help you to work through these issues a little bit at a time. This is intended to point out what lack of time management looks like and what problems it may cause. The stress can become too much and often it all spirals out of control—and this book is intended to help you proactively ensure that never happens!

If you are lacking time management in any capacity then it may seem as though you can get it under control. Usually though it starts with a general lack of control, manifests into stress and worry, then becomes a constant fear that results in lack of productivity, lack of focus, health problems, and even depression.

This just goes to show that the way in which you manage your time can be tremendously important. So if you never realized the value of time management before, it's time to get a hold of this and to use it to help you move towards a better future—it's time to break the cycle once and for all and I will help you to do just that!

Why You Need to Change Your Ways To Eliminate The Stress

If you're like most people then you probably don't think that you need to change it up. You probably think that you can handle it all and that you've done fine thus far. Most of us tend to brush off the need to take care of ourselves or manage our stress, but that can be a huge mistake. If you feel like you are in control or that you can handle it, take a step back to gain perspective and try to see if this is really true.

Most of us can stand to improve when it comes to managing our time. The reality is that there is always going to be stress in life, but it's up to us to learn how to manage it. A big part of that is working to eliminate the source of the stress—and that ties very nicely into effective time management! When you can learn to maximize your time each day and you can get rid of distractions and focus on being truly productive, then there are so many great advantages to that.

We Can All Stand To Improve In This Area If We're Really Honest

If you need convincing that you need to change your ways, I have a few. This is just hitting the surface in what you need to do to take control of things and why time management is so vital to life. Sure we all think that we have it under control, but if you are really honest with yourself then changing your ways really CAN improve your quality of life and add to your balance.

Here are just a few ways that the lack of time management and excessive stress can really hurt you and why change is essential moving forward.

- Little by little, the stress of not having enough time to get things done can chip away at you: If you don't believe it you will start to feel the negative effects of this over time. Stress seems very much like an obscure thing at first, but after awhile it starts to wear away at your mental and physical health.

    When you don't have enough time to get everything done you start to internalize that stress. This all adds up to decreased productivity and worse yet, it ends up causing you issues such as stomach problems, trouble focusing or being productive, anxiety disorders, depression, weight gain or weight loss, and worse. So the more that the stress is present, the more that this is taking its toll on you just a little bit at a time.

- If you don't take control over these bad habits, they will take control of you: Yes the bad habits that you have fallen into are going to get the best of you. Again not a scare tactic, but rather just reality. If you don't learn to effectively manage your time, the work will pile up even more. Your family and life responsibilities will become overwhelming.

    You will become moody, withdrawn, frustrated, and generally have a hard time in coping. This isn't an ideal scenario in any way! So if you want to remain in control and be productive, then you need to stay ahead of it. This is how to make your life better and how to achieve true balance—so head in the right direction by staying positive and focused!

- The only way to be truly productive and achieve a healthy and balanced lifestyle, is to change your ways for the better: Recognizing that you have problems in this area is the first and most important step. If you want to get to better days, more productivity, and really take a stand in your life then you will learn how to make effective changes now. It may be scary and feel overwhelming, but just take it one step at a time. This book will help you to create techniques that truly work, give you helpful tips, tactics, and ultimately ensure that you are more productive and truly balanced!

Take Over!

"Don't spend time beating on a wall, hoping to transform it into a door."
— Coco Chanel

Do you find yourself overwhelmed by the number of tasks that need to be accomplished at work each day? Do you feel that you have not done your part as an employee or as a boss due to small attention to details?
Are files on your table piling up because of unexpected situations and different distractions that surround you? Is your lack of organization something that you are constantly trying to defend or worrying about on your own? Are you spreading yourself to thin to try and do everything?

Well, worry no more. There are several ways to avoid these types of situations. If you follow them carefully, it will help you improve your time management skills plus it can save you from stress and fatigue that can lead to serious illnesses.

Don't feel bad or focus too much on what you have done wrong up until now, just be ready to take control back and make this work for you!

Pulling It All Together

These are the things you can achieve when you have already learned how to manage your time wisely:

- Eliminate Procrastination
- Meet Deadlines
- Avoid Distractions
- Get More Accomplished Throughout Your Day
- Better Productivity

- Peaceful State of Mind
- More Relaxation Time
- Time for sports, hobby or travelling
- The most obvious one – Achieve your Goals!

Time Management skill take time to develop and establish. It is also a craft that is unique for everyone. The best thing to do is to try several different approaches until something sticks to your brain and, eventually, becomes part of your daily routine.

It's important to remember that everyone has different things that work. Though there are plenty of different organizational methods out there, you need to figure out what works best for you. The key is to take control back and to put forth the effort. Once you do that then there's no stopping you!

You MUST stay true to managing your TIME!

Here are 10 awesome tips to get you on top of your game

1. **To Do List:** Write down as many tasks as you can in your planner or notebook, or even on your Smartphone or a recorder. If you don't carry one, start now. Personally, I prefer a Smartphone so that you can carry it anywhere and everywhere you go.

   The idea is that you write down what you need to accomplish. This serves as a visual reminder and ensures that you stay on task. You are sure to revise it as you move along, but the point is that you have it done.

   Keep your TO DO LIST simple by using keywords and in short phrases because having to look at a long list is overwhelming and, oftentimes, discouraging.

2. **Utilizing Dead Time:** Using walking, driving and breaks to think or plan on things you can do for the day is a great thing. Do not use your "Dead Times" during work or school to think about what to do the next few weeks.

   Rather, use it as a small time to reflect on what you have done for the day and what else you can do. Also, think about what your goals are for tomorrow and which tasks to do first. Learn how to prioritize.

This is productivity at its best, for when you effectively use your time to get things done then you are successful. If you can keep a notebook or other planning tool with you, then you can master anything that may come up and always capture a thought or plan.

3. **Give Yourself a Pat on the Back:** Whenever you have successfully accomplished a task, make sure to take the time to reward yourself. You can give yourself a cup of coffee in a coffee shop, an hour of television time, or just a snooze.

   Do whatever will make you feel that you have done a good job. This is not fluff but rather positive reinforcement at its best. If you want to keep being productive, then you have to feel good about what you have done and also take the time to refresh a bit.

   As Clockwork Orange author Anthony Burgess' used the "Martini Method" to get things done. Burgess set a goal of 1,000 words per day.

   When he finished his word count, he'd relax with a martini and take the day off. A Martini might not be applicable to some but I guess you already get the idea.

4. **Focus and Concentrate:** Our minds work most efficiently when we are focused. As we all know multitasking is a disadvantage to productivity because we need to do several things at the same time, thus making it very difficult to perfect each and every task.

   If instead you were to concentrate on what you need to get done at the moment and really concentrate on that, then you are sure to be more productive overall. At times, it may seem like a more efficient way to do things, but it probably is not. Focus on one thing and get it done—then take on the next task when you are ready for it.

5. **Avoid Procrastination at All Costs:**
Procrastination is the action of delaying and postponing something. When you want to be productive and you want to save as much time as possible, procrastination should be avoided at all costs.

It is the ultimate productivity-killer, yet so many of us are guilty of being procrastinators. This may be because we assume that we have plenty of time to get things done.

It may be because we simply can't focus until the deadline is upon us. Whatever the reason we need to really teach ourselves not to procrastinate and to work on things a little at a time. This will not only help us to be productive, but also stay away from the things that hold us back.

6. **Set Personal Deadlines:** No one likes deadlines nor due dates. They cause a lot of stress, frustration, irritation, and worst, fatigue. A guaranteed way to eliminate some stress is to set your own personal deadlines to all the tasks you have to do for a given time.

Be realistic but demanding to yourself. Challenge yourself to beat the deadline and reward yourself for the difficult challenges you have accomplished. It will save you time and make you more productive. Just be sure to check your list and write a star on every finished task.

7. **Delegate Responsibilities:** Do not be afraid to delegate tasks as it is not common for a person to

take on more than what he can handle. Do not underestimate your colleague's ability to finish a task.

It will improve their capabilities to work effectively on a team and it will also enhance the team's commitment to each other. Sometimes you have to recognize your own shortcomings or time commitments, so if you don't have time to get it all done you need to be honest about that.

Delegation makes you a better leader and ensures that the work gets done right. Though it's often hard to give work to somebody else, it will benefit you in the long run. If you think he is not ready for the job, then guide him or make a walkthrough process. It will increase your team's productivity, your ability to lead, and the person's work ethic.

8. **Be Ambitious – Dream Big:** In our everyday dreads of life, we can often lose sight of our specific goals. Setting up a long term planner/scheduler will help you envision your long term goals and realize your current objectives. Don't be afraid to reach for what you really want—just go for it!

    Whenever you find yourself thinking "Why am I putting myself through this amount of work right now? I could be home watching "The Walking Dead." It's all about the big picture, and that's the reason you do all of this.

    Just take a look at your long term planner/scheduler and you'll be reminded of paying your utilities, insurance, mortgage, car payment or saving up enough for your children's college tuition fees. Remember to go over your long term planner/scheduler monthly to keep it up-to-date.

9. **Teamwork:** This tip works hand-in-hand with Tip #7. Although giving up responsibilities is a scary and risky thought for some, it is an effective method to increase the average of team productivity. It's also a necessity if you truly want to be a leader!

    Make sure the team goals are clear and everyone knows who is responsible for which given tasks. Make sure all lines of communications are open and not cluttered, and thus avoid misunderstandings. Delegate the tasks to those who are suited for it. Know that everyone has strengths and weaknesses, and you need to find yours and those of your team members.

    However, it is better for the team to work flexibly. Create a walkthrough process on all your given tasks so everyone can follow and eventually, everyone on your team will be capable of doing everything that needs to be done. One person doing the job is good but two or more is better.

10. **Say NO to Burnout:** Burnout is a physical or emotional exhaustion, especially as a result of long term stress. At work, burnouts occur when your body and mind can no longer keep up with the tasks you demand them to. Needless to say this is counterproductive and will never end well!

    This all results in emotional conflicts such as losing your confidence and self-esteem. Don't force yourself to do the impossible. Know when you are getting close to the point of burnout, and really learn to listen to your body and your mind for signs.

    Delegate time for important things, but always factor in time for relaxation for you to do a reality check. Review your recent accomplishments, and feel good about them. This is the best way to regain your confidence back. It will also increase your productivity and work ethic.

How Getting Organized Can Add More Time To Your Day

You may not realize it, but you are actually going to add more time to your day if you work at getting organized. This is something that causes a lot of people to stand up and take notice. When you consider that the benefits outweigh the work that you put into all of this, it's well worth it to work at your time management skills. Becoming a more organized individual can add so much to your life that you will wonder why you never did this before.

Though many argue that getting organized takes too much time out of their day, you stand to gain so many wonderful benefits that it's well worth it. Sure you are going to have to put forth some effort and some time into all of this, but it shows itself in true productivity. You won't feel stressed, you will improve your health, and therefore the investment into your well being is worth it alone.

You Add Time and Energy To Your Day—Plus So Much More

If you don't believe that time management and organization can benefit you, here are just a few ways that show differently. The initial investment of time into getting organized will far outweigh the drawbacks—and you will come to see that these benefits are immeasurable.

- Your mental well being will improve when you are organized: You start to feel more energized and more focused when you get organized. It's almost as if there is more of a purpose to your day. You are much happier, balanced, and relaxed because you know that you have a plan by which to get it all done. Though it does take effort to get organized at first, you will start to see that the benefits to your state of mind and mental well being make it totally worth it.

- Your physical well being will become remarkably better as your stress level will be down: You no longer feel as though you are literally carrying the weight of the world on your shoulders. You are relaxed in every sense of the word and that really improves your physical health. You are able to stand with better posture, you don't get the anxiety that you used to, you no longer have stomach aches, or any other health problems that the stress was causing you before. This is how it all works when you can cope each day, be productive, and don't feel that all too familiar stress that you are used to.

- You will actually be able to get more done as you have a path to work towards: Creating your own path towards productivity means that you get more done in a day. You are essentially buying yourself more time, strange as it sounds. This results in you having a better capability to handle what comes your way.

    You are also more adept at working through challenges that come up unexpectedly. You get more done when you have a plan, and though that plan may take some time out of your schedule it's going to pay off big time. You need to plot out that path and that's where some good organization really comes into play.

- You maximize your day and have added priority and structure to your plan of attack: From the start of your day to the finish, you have some sort of structure to work within. This framework helps to keep you on track and ensures that you have something to guide you. In so doing this you also attach priorities to each of the items on here and really have some great ideas of how to get everything done within a day. Though this may have sounded like a daunting task in the past, it no longer is because now you have it all spelled out for you.

The "to do list", the time savers, and all of the ideas and priorities of what you need to get done each day will all contribute to this in a very positive way. The investment of time to get organized and be productive ultimately ensures that you maximize every ounce of your time, and this is what helps you to work towards short and long term goals. This will create a much healthier, happier, and balanced lifestyle in the end—therefore showing that organization really pays off in the long run!

What Effective Time Management Can Add To Your Life

Have you ever felt that you wanted more out of your day? Do you ever feel as though you're running in place and yet not know how to get out of that rut? Are you fearful that your lack of time management and organization can hurt you in the long run? If you want to take your life back, then learning to manage your time effectively is the first and most important step in the process.

Perhaps you know of somebody who is truly organized and therefore wonder what their secret is. How do they have the time to invest into getting organized? Isn't it hard enough to get through the day much less to have a time and place for everything? What you may not realize is that time management can add so many wonderful elements to your life.

This Is An Investment That Pays Off Tremendously

Sure it's an investment of time and effort to get started, but it's going to help you so much in the long run. Not only that but you are going to be much more focused and this will become routine for you before you even realize it. So if you needed motivation before, consider what you will gain through getting organized. There are so many wonderful ways that you can add back to your life through this minimal investment of time.

To spell it out sometimes helps you to feel convinced, and so here we look at what the specific benefits of time management can be. These are the ways that you can add to your life and benefit yourself in the short and long term, all by getting organized and learning to better manage your time.

- You will be far more productive: When you have a plan and a means by which to get things done, then you are automatically going to be more productive. So the more that you stay with your plan and your given organization method, the more productive that you will be.

    You are writing down your tasks and therefore able to manage them better. You know what you have coming, you are prepared, and you can even handle the unforeseen better. So in the end making lists and getting organized can give you more time back in your day, and really enhance your overall productivity which is an amazing benefit.

- You will enjoy better health in the short and long term: When you stay ahead of the tasks at hand, then you can relax and take care of yourself. You aren't always caught in a tailspin and therefore are more cognizant of what your body and your mind are telling you.

    If you need to slow down a bit or if you need to recharge, you have a better way to do so. Not only that but you aren't run down and suffering from a compromised immune system because you are able to get everything done in a day. This is a more indirect benefit of time management that few realize and yet it has so many positive implications. So the more that you invest into managing your time, the better it will serve you as you move into the future.

- You will learn to manage your stress and eliminate common sources of it: You aren't as stressed out when you have a plan. You can work through the items on your list and priorities in order. You aren't worrying about running behind because you have a method by which to attack everything. The common sources of stress in the past no longer have a hold on you.

So learning to stay focused and finding ways to manage your stress will benefit you, and it all starts with time management. You won't feel that pressure and you will get more done in a day, all of which lessens the anxiety and puts you in a better place.

- You will feel more at ease and in control of what you have to do: You feel more confident when you are productive and in charge of your day. You are focused on the task at hand and prepared for what is to come. You can take on the unforeseen and it doesn't bother you as it once did. You are at ease, you are much happier, you are more balanced, and you ultimately become a much better version of yourself. All by managing your time and getting organized---there is no doubt that this is an investment well worth making into your health and well being!

Outcomes of Poor Time Management

When time management is not applied to our daily lives, stress can occur and it can harm our health when not relieved for a long period of time. Stress is the body's reaction to any change that requires an adjustment or response. It is actually part of our everyday life to help us to be motivated in resolving an issue, keep us alert when there is danger and lets us meet our deadlines.

Though stress is inevitable, feeling stress without any real relief can lead to very harmful long term effects. The stress easily creeps into our body, and also begins to cause problems with our mental and emotional health as well. If you don't get a handle on your stress and it becomes long term, it can seriously interfere with your job, family life, and health.

Research also suggests that stress can bring about or worsen certain symptoms or diseases. When we are stressed out, we tend to get into the bad habits of smoking, drinking or maybe taking drugs. These things can get our body and health into serious trouble. The direct and indirect effects of stress are far reaching, and so it's time to get a handle on this.

How Stress Affects The Body

You may not feel it as you're going through it, but stress is taking its toll on you each and every day. Many people feel that they can handle the stress that they are given and be perfectly fine. They feel that they have it under control and therefore don't put much of an emphasis on effective stress management. Then suddenly it can hit you like a ton of bricks.

If you don't believe it, then all you have to do is look at some of the most common symptoms of stress. These can be eye opening, for even if they are not directly affecting you now they may someday. So to fully understand, here are the most common symptoms of stress:

- Fast heartbeat
- Headache
- Stiff neck/tight shoulders
- Back pain
- Fast breathing
- Sweaty/sweating
- Upset stomach
- Nausea
- Diarrhea

Over time, stress can affect our:

Immune System. If you are continuously feeling stress for a long period of time, you are much more likely to get sick more often than usual. Stress can decrease the level of strength of your immune system.

Heart. Stress is directly connected to **high blood pressure**, and to any heart related illness. So too much stress can lead to these diseases.

Muscles. Continuous stress can lead to neck, **shoulder**, and lower **back pain**s. Stress can make rheumatism and arthritis go from bad to worse.

Stomach. If you have stomach problems, (such as GERD or an ulcer) stress can make your symptoms far worse.

Reproductive organs. Stress is associated with low **fertility**, **erection problems**, problems during **pregnancy**, and painful menstrual periods.

Lungs. Stress can make symptoms of **asthma** and other lung diseases terrifyingly horrible.

Skin. Skin problems such as **acne** and psoriasis are worsened by stress.

Stress can affect your thoughts and emotions. You might notice signs of stress in the way you think, act, and feel. You may feel irritable and unable to deal with small problems. You are also more likely to be frustrated and short tempered. You are not able to focus on your task, you feel so restless, and you worry too much about small things. You feel overwhelmed and unable to cope.

However some people handle stress differently than others do. Well it is because we have different ways to deal with it based on our personality. How we are brought up by our families, our coping strategies, and how many people are there to support us all play a part. So many things within our lives contribute to our ability to cope with stress and lessen it.

It is very important that in our lowest times we have someone we can talk to and who will listen to us to ease our pain, frustration and anger. If they are not around, we can resort to our favorite sport, game, hobby or even meditation to overcome the challenges of life as we move forward. Whatever method works best for you, it's important to find productive ways of dealing with stress so that you can function at your best.

Eating Your Way Out of Stress

Many contribute stress for their emotional eating habits and therefore turn to food for comfort. Though you want to find other healthy ways of eliminating the stress, there are some foods that can naturally help to balance you out. These can offer you a healthy way of lessening the stress and achieving better health in the process.

The foods that have a calming effect include:

- Whole Grains: They provide a great natural energy and they also help to release hormones that make you feel relaxed and calm

- Blueberries: They are rich in antioxidants which not only help to contribute to a boosted immune system, but also help your mood

- Almonds: They are high in zinc which has a direct effect on improving your mood

- Avocado: They are a good fat and rich in Omega 3 fatty acids, and they may help you to feel more balanced

- Dark Chocolate: In proper portions, the antioxidants within this can help you to feel calm, balanced, and healthier

Please refer to the end of this book (Appendix section) for additional list of foods and recipes.

Stress Management Techniques

Do you really want to bring undue problems and illnesses to your mental and physical well-being? Well the more stressed you are the more problems you will have. From the inside to the out there are many illnesses and diseases that come about because of stress and anxiety you put on yourself.

Look at it this way:

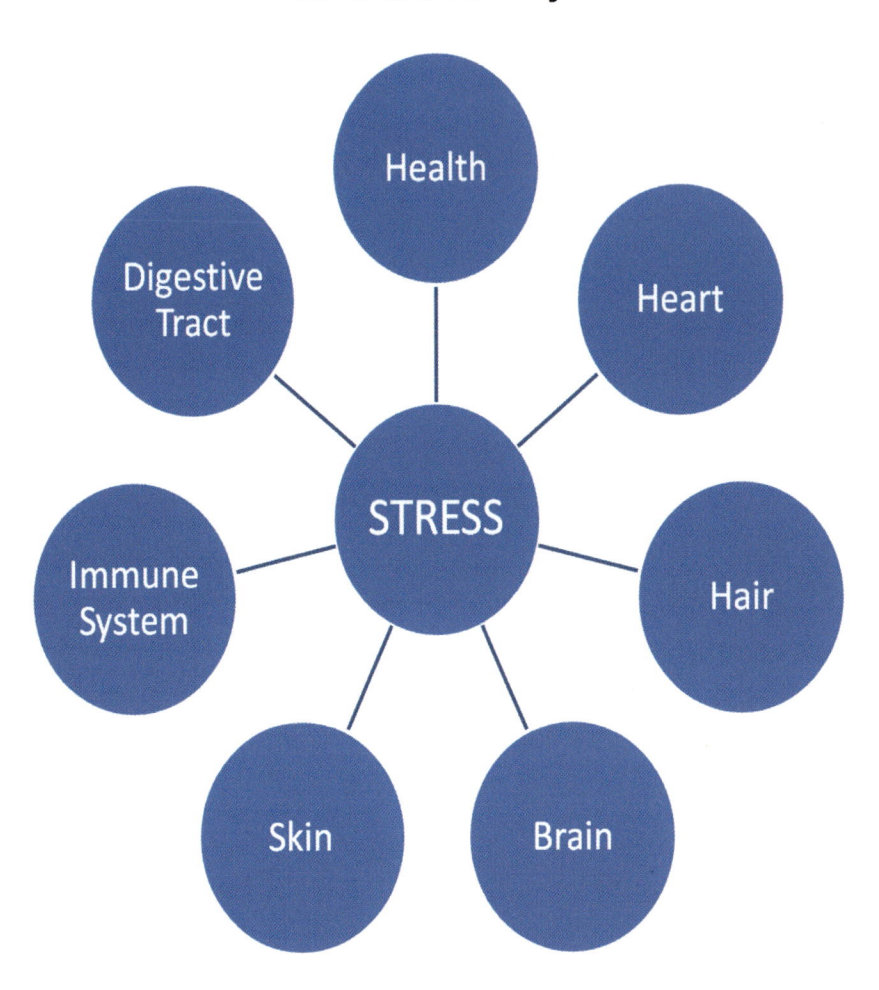

- Health
- Heart
- Hair
- Brain
- Skin
- Immune System
- Digestive Tract

STRESS

Stress, anxiety, burned out, tense, fatigued, exhausted, whatever you are feeling that is bringing you down must be fixed in order to enjoy better health. No matter if it is emotional or physical stress or a combination learning to control it and/or prevent it in the first place is key. Stress effects everyone, from young to old to rich to poor, whether it is mild or out of control, we all have it. There are so many symptoms associated with stress and whatever illness or sickness you may have stress can worsen it. Stress can cause weight gain and pain attacks. Although high blood pressure or heart disease is not caused by stress, stress can worsen the progression. Chronic stress can weaken your immune system and deplete your body of vitamins which can leave you vulnerable to colds and infections, wounds not healing quickly, not responding to vaccinations, etc…

Whether you have a support group or benefit from stress relieving techniques on your own you must find effective ways to cope with stress. Here are some tips and techniques to help:

- Exercise
- Meditation
- Yoga
- Breathing
- Time Management
- Organization
- Stress-Busting Foods
- Herbal Supplements
- Adequate Sleep

Please refer to the Appendix Chapter, Yoga and Breathing Techniques, illustrated by Tameisha Shevelle Harrington

How Much Is Your Time Worth? (Define The Cost Of Your Time)

"Until you value yourself, you won't value your time. Until you value your time, you will not do anything with it."
-M. Scott Peck

Establish your Priorities

This part will help you identify what you need to do first and what can wait. All of us have this wrong impression of what we really need from just what we want. Sometimes our desires give us the thought that our wants are our needs, which always gets us into trouble in dealing with our budgets. This highly affects the time that we are supposed to have paid the bills and the time that we are supposed to be working on the next budget for the next cut off.

Make a list of what are needs and wants to identify what you need to prioritize. Make a timeline for your priorities, put it on a calendar, notebook or Smartphone to make it happen. Review the list monthly or even weekly to keep it up-to-date. Always remember, when needs are satisfied, then you have all the time for what you really want.

Calculating What Your Cost Is

Appraising this number is quite easy. First of all, you need to know how much you're earning annually. Don't include any investment returns or things of that nature. Now subtract every single extra cost incurred such as utilities, mortgages, school fees, transportation costs (gas, car maintenance and repair, etc.), meals, snacks, coffee, office supplies, gifts, and so forth.

The total should be a month's worth divide it by the number of days you are working then multiply it by the number of weeks in a year you are working. When you can see this all in print then it makes much more sense. You want to be forthcoming with each number to get the most out of this exercise.

Expenses	Amount	Total
Electricity	$ 250.00	$ 1,116.24
Water		
Phone/Internet	60.50	
Cable		
Transportation (car/gas/repair)	99.99	
	55.75	
	650.00	
Groceries	$ 500.00	$ 2,670.00
Meals/Snacks	170.00	
Travel (hotel/meals/transportation)	2,000.00	
Mortgage	$ 750.00	$ 3,570.00
Insurance	320.00	
School	3,000.00	

TOTAL: $ 7,856.24/Month

Then estimate the exact hours you devote to your employment each year. You are maybe working between 40-50 hours a week for 48-52 weeks a year. You also have to write the number of hours you spend driving or riding public transportation going to work, the extra time you work outside the office, business travel and all the other stuff you do outside the office but it is still working. Again, if you don't know how much time you invest, make a week's estimate and multiply by 52, or make a month's estimate and multiply by 12.

When you have these numbers, take the real amount of your salary and divide it by the real number of hours you put in for your job. The total will be your worth per hour using your most recent employment as your touchstone.

Take time to write it down on a napkin or piece a paper during your coffee breaks, it will shock you that it will only take you 10 minutes of your time to actually do this.

Know your Strengths and Weaknesses

We all have our strengths and also must identify and accept our weaknesses. By assessing ourselves we can find out what we can do best with the least amount of effort. We can also identify problem areas or things that we are not too good at, which usually causes a small problem achieving it.

By doing so, you can now concentrate and focus on what you need to do on things that you are good at. You can work at delegating the things you know you can't do well to people who happen to be good at that task. You will obtain a faster, effective and efficient processing system not to mention that it will make you happier and satisfied with yourself, thus causing less stress.

The key here is to list your strengths and weaknesses on paper or in a notebook, and make notes on how you can enhance your strengths and how to improve your weaknesses. You can also make a chart to show your development. In this way, you will be able to see how far you have gone.

Remember that strengths and weaknesses are internal factors that you may have a direct hand in making and improving. The weather and vehicular traffic are things on the external side. To help you with identifying your strengths and weaknesses, you may refer to some of these questions as a starting guide.

- What skills and capabilities do I possess?
- What activities do I do the best / I don't do too well?
- In a thinking, planning and production process, what area or step am I best / I need improvement or help?
- What tasks am I happy to do?
- What weaknesses do I have?
- What tasks do I feel frustrated doing?

After identifying your strengths and weaknesses, find external factors that you may use to your advantage by using your strengths more and minimizing your weaknesses. For example rush hour is a big problem for delivery time and makes you frustrated and timid to do such tasks.

If it just so happens that one of your strengths is that you are an early morning riser, then you can use this for delivering the goods before rush hour allowing you to accomplish your task earlier.

This can make you more proud of your accomplishment and eliminating the idea of the frustrating and timid feeling you have regarding your delivery tasks. Guidelines to identify external factors are important and they include:

- What are obstacles that take away your focus on your strengths?
- What are the external factors that may hinder your success?
- What external factors can I use as an advantage to my strengths and weaknesses?
- What opportunities do my external factors present?

In my own opinion and based on experience, strengths are gained by improving your weaknesses. It will always be a "one step at a time" process. Along your journey to success, struggles and all sorts of obstacles will come your way no matter how systematic and organized you are.

Being prepared is not always the answer, but facing the problem itself and weighing the pros and cons is sometimes what we need to keep us stronger and wiser. It all starts by being honest with yourself, and then you can make great progress from there.

We all have areas that we excel in, and we all have areas that we need to improve upon. This is nothing to be ashamed of or to feel bad about, but rather just life. If you want to figure out where you should concentrate most of your effort then get in tune with this and use this as a journey to really explore who you are—this will all tie into more effective time management and greater productivity in the end!

Avoiding Distractions and Focusing On What Really Matters—True Prioritization

"Circumstances may cause interruptions and delays, but never lose sight of your goal."
-Mario Andretti

Are you unable to concentrate on the tasks you should be doing? Are you focusing too much attention on gossip, chit chat, web surfing, and other insignificant activities? If yes, then you are letting distractions run your day.

Distraction - a thing that prevents someone from giving full attention to something else.

Focus – to pay particular attention to

The number one enemy of focus is distraction. In this chapter, we will discuss how distractions affect your success and how we can avoid it. We will also talk about the different kinds of distractions and how to deal with them.

Yes we're all guilty of giving into distractions, whether we realize it or not. We all have so many other things that can steal our attention away, and therefore these can become time suckers. We're all guilty of giving into distractions, but we need to work through them!

Be Proactive and Stay Ahead of Things

A few weeks after my high school graduation, I started to pack my things for college. I wanted to start as early as possible so as not to interrupt my long awaited month long travel vacation. I started to separate my clothes from my underwear, my socks from my hankies, and my shoes from my slip ons. I put them neatly inside my luggage in an orderly manner. I also put post its on my boxes to label them. I started with books, pillows & blankets. I was really making great progress!

After packing, I felt really accomplished that I had finished packing ahead of time, and as if I was totally ready to go to college when I got back from my vacation. This simple attitude towards your own personal things will also reflect how you work. Sounds simplistic, but think about this for a moment!

If your room is messy, there is an 80% chance that you are cramming to finish a deadline, constantly tardy, and most likely be in distress in all aspects of your life (work, family, relationship). The point here is that when one area of your life is unorganized or distracted, this tends to be an issue across other areas as well.

So if you can recognize that your patterns and habits can help to contribute to unproductive ways, then you can be more aware of it. When you notice the typical distractions then you can do your best to avoid them. Sure it may force you to see things that you don't always want to see, but this is how you work towards productivity in the end.

How To Ensure You Stay Ahead of the Game

1. Do not procrastinate: Though we all may be guilty of it, recognize it when you're doing it. Don't put things off when you can instead get them done. Find a way to compartmentalize so that you can get things done now instead of waiting for later and then adding a whole level of unnecessary stress.

2. Keep a record or a list: If you have a visual reminder of what you have to get done, then it's a lot harder to ignore it. Write it down, keep it handy, and then ensure that you cross things off as you move along.

3. Write it down or put it on your Smartphone: There are no rules to how you go about writing down what you must get done, just be sure that you do it. If you take the time to write down each and every activity or task then you are sure to keep up with the overall flow. Not only will this help you to stay productive, but it's also a lot harder to get distracted when you see what's at hand.

4. Create a timeline: Don't just say you'll get it done at some point in time as that will never happen. Set a realistic but detailed timeline so that you can work towards your goals. If you can do this then you will be much more focused and distractions won't get in your way.

5. Give yourself a deadline: Along the same lines, set yourself a workable deadline. Something that you can work towards and keep in front of you always. Some

tangible date or idea of when you can get the work accomplished. The more detail, the better in the end!

6. Push yourself harder and be smarter about how to get the job done: Don't get lazy but rather stay motivated. Keep pushing yourself and put a little pressure on yourself to get things done right. Always keep your eye on the deadline and you will stay motivated.

Identify Distractions

When we are distracted, we lose our focus thus we lose sight of our goal. It doesn't matter if it is someone who keeps disturbing you during work, or an errand you need to do. The point is that a distraction can be anything that is keeping you from getting the work done in the end, and that's why you must identify it and therefore work past it.

Distractions are distractions, and if we give way to these kinds of things we are going to lose more time than we can imagine. You want to pinpoint what your most common sources of distractions are, so that you can then work to avoid them. Here are some of the most common sources of distractions, and surely one or more of these may apply to you.

Common Sources of Distractions:

1. Chit chat or gossip
2. Watching a movie /video during work hours
3. Browsing social networking sites (Facebook, Photobucket, etc…)
4. Taking too many coffee or cigarette breaks
5. Worrying too much that you will never get the job done on time
6. Boss putting too much pressure on you, and you crumbling under this pressure
7. Taking calls or emails that you don't need for the work that you are doing
8. Taking on personal tasks when you really need to focus on the professional tasks at hand
9. Getting caught up in something completely unrelated to try and problem solve, and then losing sight of what you are supposed to be doing

10. Giving into the desire to be doing anything else or being anywhere else, rather than completing the work

When we get distracted, it takes time to get back to what we were doing. We need to be in a state of mind that we are ready to do something, or else we will just end up messing it up or doing it halfway. I really believe that the level of focus we have will all be gone once interruptions occur.

I guess the best way to deal with it is to brush them off your path, and remember that distractions are challenges to get us ahead of our schedules. If you don't know how to handle them, you'll end up doing more work with less rest and a lot more stress.

Be In Control

Planning your day is one step to take control of your time. It can greatly help in spacing things out and being on time on your "things to do". Whether it is a meeting, a task or a simple snack break it helps you get organized. As you make and study your list, please understand that you have the same amount of time like everyone else, do not overbook the impossible tasks and commitments. It makes you respect your time as well as that of others, plus it also makes you feel more accomplished by getting the "check sign" on those to do items rather than scrambling around rushing to every meeting.

Know what the REAL things are to do. You may find it "a must" that you visit a social website first thing in the morning to get the latest updates of your virtual friends. The truth however is that the time spent in preparing your own breakfast will not only give you proper nutrition for the day, but also saves you time and money from grabbing something unhealthy but convenient on the way to work.

What I mean is you always have something to be done in a certain period of time, and you need to choose what will benefit you the most. It does not mean that you have to give up your "social relevance" in the virtual world, but logging in only on a weekend would not hurt too much. Doing something like this may also make way to have more time for you to really meet up with your friends and show them a healthier looking you!

Take control of your everyday distractions. Saying "No" to a colleague or a friend when all they do is chit chat/gossip. Do not make yourself available at all times. Try as much as possible to avoid being caught up by saying "hey, I need to finish this first, let me talk to you in a bit." By doing that, you are taking priority of your job not of your interruptions.

Be in control over you what you get done in a day and what you allow yourself to get distracted by. This is a choice and a time investment, but it's going to really work to make you more productive in the end!

Getting Back On Track After a Crazy or Offbeat Day

It happens to the best of us and even with the best of intentions—we fall off track and give into a crazy day! In spite of the best planning, we fall into old traps and give into that lack of productivity that we know all too well. Just when you thought that you were getting organized and really making the most of your time, this can come as a very unwelcome obstacle and a frustrating one at that.

As you will see in future chapters, there are a number of apps and helpful tools that can help you to be productive. Even with the best tools however, sometimes you fall off track and may feel sure that there is no getting back from it. The traps still remain, so how can we be sure to overcome them and get back to productive habits? How can we ultimately ensure that we don't give into past bad habits and end up back at square one?

You Need To Identify What Has Gone Wrong To Work Past Your Obstacles

In order to be your best and to really work to overcome the bad habits, you need to first be mindful of your bad habits. This takes a bit of soul searching to understand what went wrong. What served as your biggest distractions? What kept you from being organized before? Ultimately what made you into that unorganized and often chaotic person that you never want to return to?

When you can dig deep and uncover the answers to all of those questions, then you can work towards better long term solutions. So even if you had a terrible day and made all the past mistakes, here are some effective ways to get back on track and overcome this cycle once and for all.

- Recognize what went wrong and then work to avoid it in the future: There was some sort of distraction or some sort of trap that was present that you gave into. Take inventory here and really look at what caused you to choose the wrong path. Though you may not always want to admit this, being honest with yourself will help you to uncover the truth.

  Not only can that help you to provide a great overview of what caused the problem, but more importantly how to avoid it moving forward. Look at what caused the mishap or the bad day, get to the heart of it, acknowledge it, and then move on. Don't beat yourself up, but rather learn from it, so that you can avoid it in the future for good!

- Figure out how to avoid this trap, but don't beat yourself up about it: Once you can identify the problem area then you can figure out a good strategy for avoiding it in the future. It may be that you avoid the person or problem altogether. It may be that you get better at working to avoid distractions, or it may just be a matter of more self discipline. Perhaps you need to work at making a more detailed list, or maybe it's just a simple matter of staying focused on what you have to get done. Whatever went wrong can be avoided and a solution can be found, and once you put that all together you can avoid this trap for the long term.

- Get back to good habits, work to avoid distractions, and get yourself back up to speed quickly: To stay on the straight and narrow means that you get back to good habits. In the past you probably gave into the bad habits and went down the wrong path. Now you know what it takes to get and stay organized and to be productive, therefore you can create a plan for success.

Avoid those common distractions, figure out what it takes for YOU personally to get organized, and then work hard to stay on task. This will be your greatest gift in terms of productivity and you will love how this strategy creates true and long term success.

Technological Advances--Time Management Tools and Applications

"They always say time changes things, but you actually have to change them yourself."
-Andy Warhol

Techie - a technical expert, student, or enthusiast, especially in the field of electronics.

No person can argue with the numerous benefits technology has delivered to us. It has definitely allowed us to connect, perform, improve and take our resources beyond what was once unimaginable. We all make use of a broad range of tools and devices to make our lives effortlessly convenient. How many tools and apps are you currently using to optimize your time?

If you are not using any of the hundreds of apps and tools out there, you are seriously missing out. Though it may seem overwhelming, it's important to cater the products that you use around your specific needs. With so many apps to choose from, how do you know which ones to use for your particular needs? Here are the questions you need to answer in finding out which apps to use:

Where does your time go? Find an app that can help you track your time when browsing over the internet. When you see it spelled out for you to understand what is truly zapping your time away, then you can work to overcome any bad habits. This can make you realize how much time you are using by just looking around. Below is an example of a powerful tool to help you save time.

Rescue Time https://www.rescuetime.com/

If you have doubts that you are using your time wisely, this app will send you weekly reports to indicate your time thieves. It may be hard to be honest about this at first, but you will quickly see just how important being straightforward really is. You may be shocked to discover how much time you are wasting, but then you can make effective changes as necessary.

How It Works

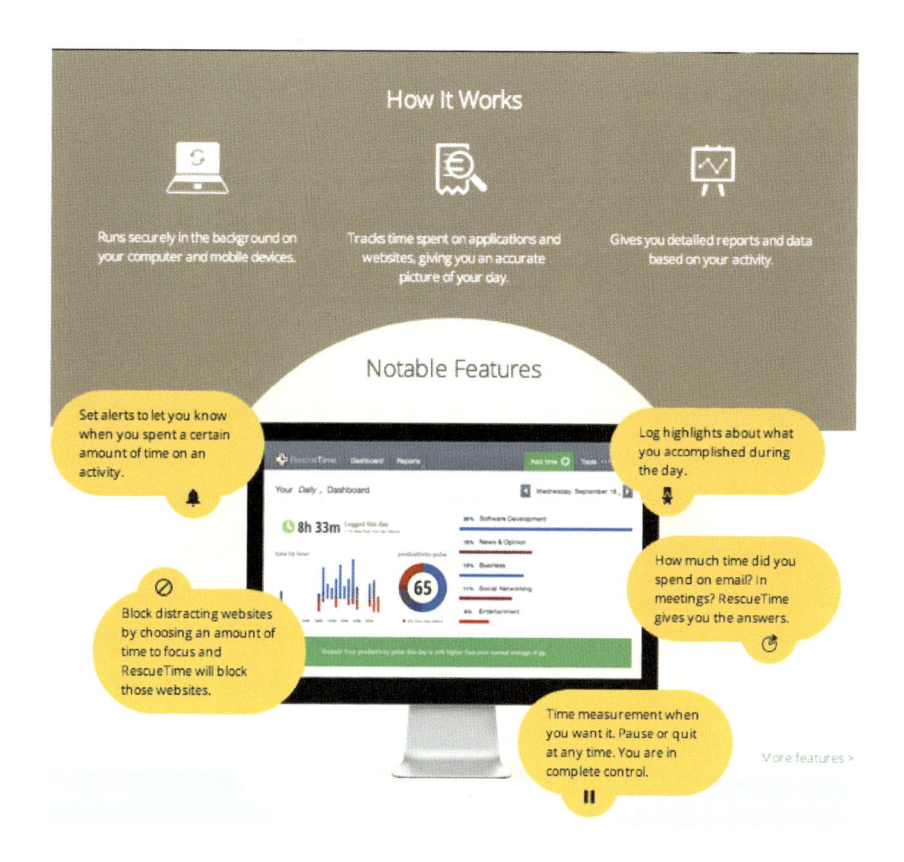

Runs securely in the background on your computer and mobile devices.

Tracks time spent on applications and websites, giving you an accurate picture of your day.

Gives you detailed reports and data based on your activity.

Notable Features

- Set alerts to let you know when you spent a certain amount of time on an activity.
- Log highlights about what you accomplished during the day.
- Block distracting websites by choosing an amount of time to focus and RescueTime will block those websites.
- How much time did you spend on email? In meetings? RescueTime gives you the answers.
- Time measurement when you want it. Pause or quit at any time. You are in complete control.

More features >

Can it manage all your tasks effectively? Always review the app's features before going for it. It should suit your everyday needs, and should have the proper features to help you remember your daily tasks. There is no need for a "one size fits all" type of approach, and you should instead find the specific apps that will benefit you the most.

Remember The Milk http://www.rememberthemilk.com/

If you are struggling to manage everything you have to do and you work with many different devices, this app is for you. It is a great free tool which is compatible with your mobile, computer, Gmail, outlook, etc.

It helps you to manage your tasks easily and reminds you of them wherever you are. From creating a simple list to helping to break down your day into manageable tasks, this is an app that can be your companion every step of the way.

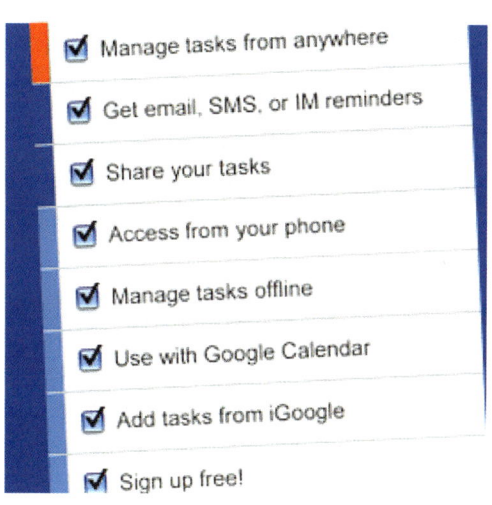

remember the milk™

- ☑ Manage tasks from anywhere
- ☑ Get email, SMS, or IM reminders
- ☑ Share your tasks
- ☑ Access from your phone
- ☑ Manage tasks offline
- ☑ Use with Google Calendar
- ☑ Add tasks from iGoogle
- ☑ Sign up free!

Can it send and receive large files? There are a lot of apps today that can help you send and receive large files such as Adobe Photoshop files or .psd. These files are stored online and you can share it with your colleagues and friends.

Dropbox http://www.dropbox.com

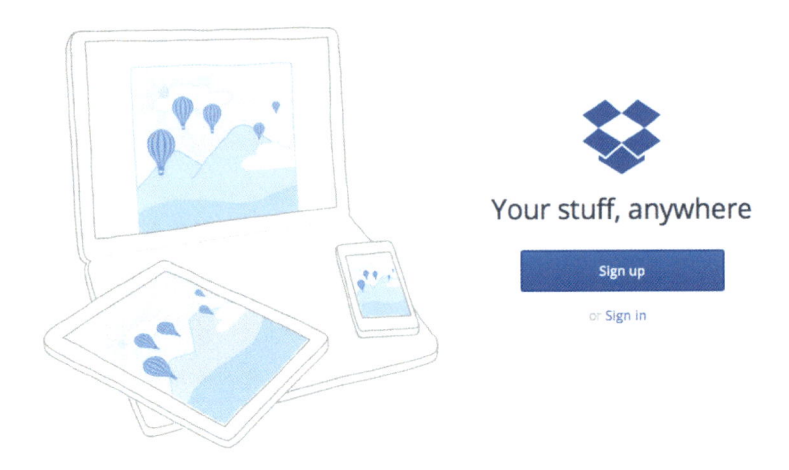

This tool can be accessed on your computer, laptop, mobile and tablets for your ultimate convenience.

Wherever you are

Put your stuff in Dropbox and get to it from your computers, phones, or tablets. Edit docs, automatically add photos, and show off videos from anywhere.

Share with confidence

Share photos with friends. Work with your team like you're using a single computer. Everything's automatically private, so you control who sees what.

Safe and secure

Even if your phone goes for a swim, your stuff is always safe in Dropbox and can be restored in a snap. Dropbox secures your files with 256-bit AES encryption and two-step verification.

Can it capture everything in one place? Here is an example of an app that can cover, basically, everything you need in one place.

Evernote http://evernote.com/

Evernote is a free productivity tool that allows you to capture all your ideas, thoughts and images in many different ways, eg, with voice, notes or images. The key here is productivity because it allows you to break down and personalize things the way it will work best for you.

You can even record your meetings, interviews, speeches and ideas, create lists, add voice or text attachments and share your files with friends. Now, you can also sync "remember the milk" with Evernote to really optimize your time.

Can it track time spent on Projects? It is very essential to track your time when you have a deadline. Projects are short-term tasks and should be accomplished within a certain period of time. Here is an app that can help you track your time spent on projects.

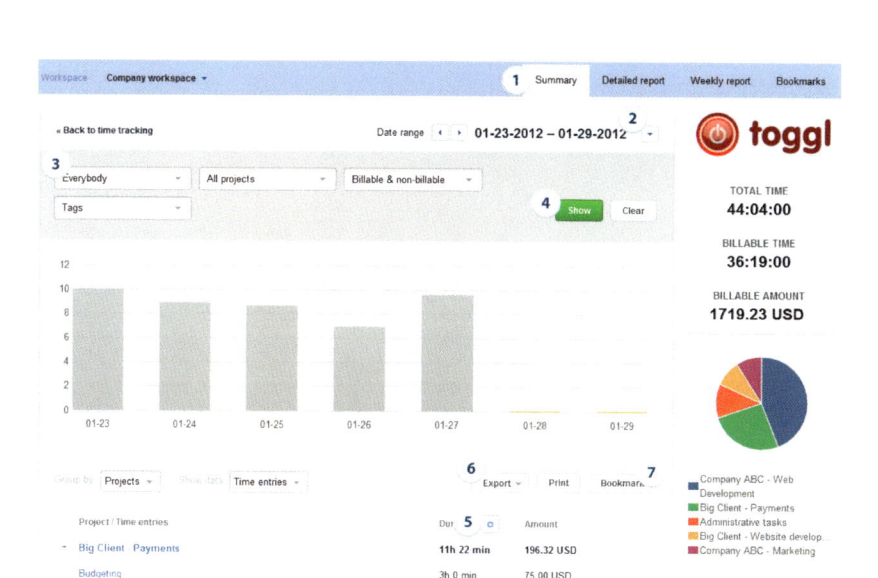

Toggl https://www.toggl.com/

This is a great alternative to timesheets if you need to track how much time you spend on different projects. Effective time management starts with being clear on exactly how much time you actually spend on your projects and tasks, and then analyze how you can manage them more effectively.

Seeing the breakdown in chart form or attaching very real and legitimate deadlines to all that you do will ultimately help you to stay on track. It's a lot harder to ignore your tasks when they are in black and white before you—this is the key to better productivity!

Do you want to back up and sync your files effortlessly?

Apps can also come in handy as a portable external hard drive. Here is a good app that can sync your files whenever, wherever..

Syncback Freeware
http://www.2brightsparks.com/syncback/

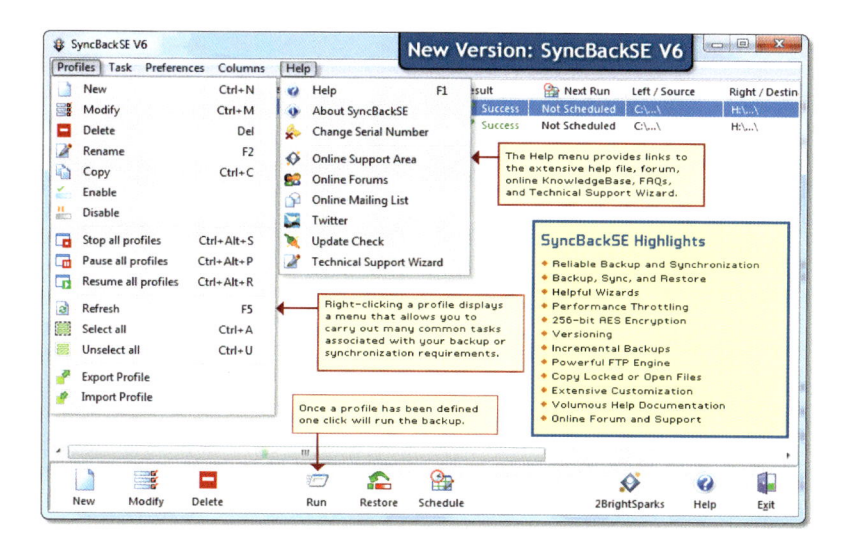

This free software allows you to back up, restore and synchronize your files easily. It not only saves you time now, but also in the future. If you have never backed up your files before, you should certainly not overlook this pivotal tool.

There are also a couple of apps that can help you remove distractions and increase your attention span. Here are great examples of these apps:

Pocketfree

https://itunes.apple.com/en/app/pocket-formerly-read-it-later/id309601447?mt=8

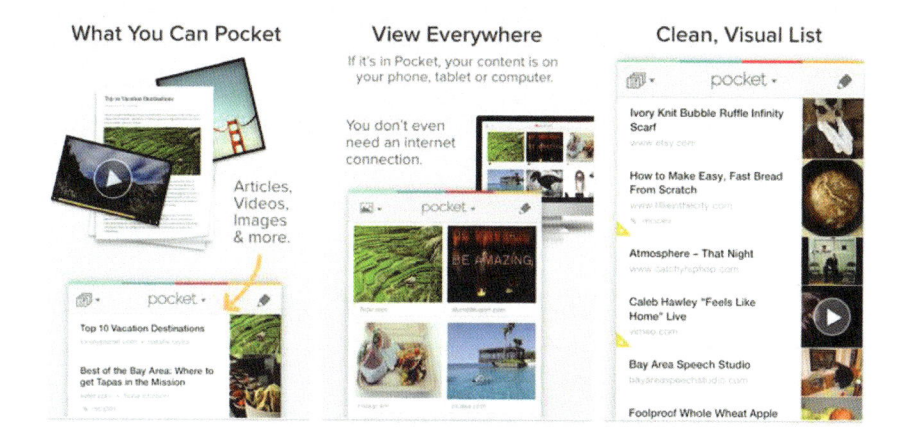

When you are surfing the web, it is so easy to get distracted by enticing websites. Use this tool to save your 'finds' to access and read later on at a convenient time which will not impact your work.

Focus at will https://www.focusatwill.com/music

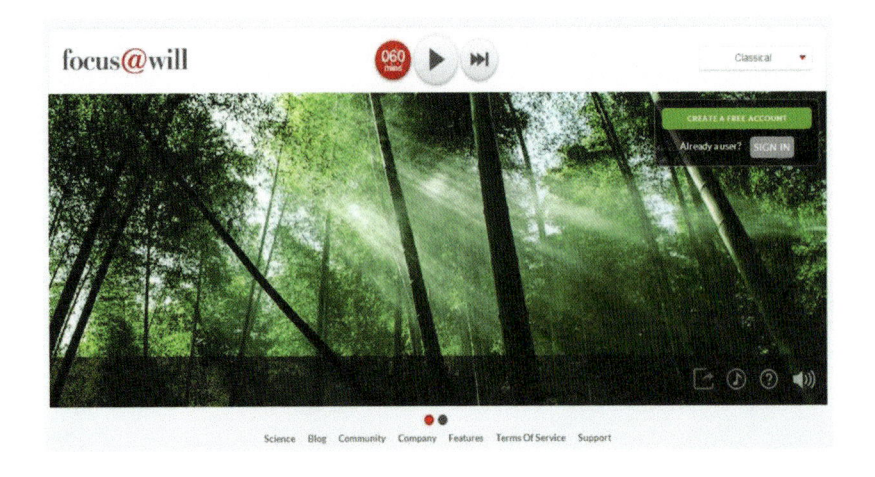

This amazing app combines neuroscience and music to boost your productivity. It is possible to increase your attention span by up to 400%! Ideal for those who find it difficult to focus while studying, working or reading, because now you can get more done in a more streamlined manner.

A BIGGER LIST OF RESOUCES IS AVAILABLE IN APPENDIX SECTION

Creating an Effective Daily Schedule That Works For You

There is no "one size fits all" type of schedule that works the same for everyone. The truth is though that we can all benefit from having a schedule to help guide us through our days. If you have just been winging it or live only by your scheduled appointments for the day, then it's time to make some effective changes. A well planned schedule can truly ensure that you get everything done and enjoy greater productivity in the process.

It's always helpful to plan out your schedule the night before when you have the opportunity. If you put in a few minutes each day to plan ahead then it will make things run much more smoothly. It's important to note that the unforeseen will often come about and can throw you for a loop. If however you have properly planned out your day, then you can still work through those circumstances and make the best of them—thus still enjoying productivity!

Planning Out Your Day Helps You To Navigate Through Anything

It may again sound like more work to create a schedule each and every day, but this is yet another investment into yourself. You can only get more organized when you have a schedule. You are accountable, you have spelled out the tasks at hand, you have prioritized as a result of this, and therefore you have a wonderful plan to help move you forward. This is a good reminder if you feel frustrated or challenged with creating a schedule at first.

If you find that you need a little push or motivation with creating a schedule, consider the benefits. Here is how to go about creating an effective schedule and why it can benefit you so greatly.

- Being realistic with your time constraints and centering a schedule around this accordingly: We all have a lot to do and when you are realistic with those time constraints then you can get a whole lot more done. It may sound counterintuitive or exhausting to spell everything out, but it will always work to your favor.

  Your schedule can center around the absolute necessities of what you need to get done and then attach the appropriate amount of time to such activities. Though you might think that this will create an unrealistic or frustrating point of view, you will be surprised at just how it helps you to stay on task and work through things one activity at a time each day.

- Carving out time for all activities, personal or professional, for a thorough overview: This is a schedule to get you through each and every thing that you have planned for the day. If you know that you have your son's soccer game in the evening, put it on the schedule. If you know that you have calls to return in the afternoon, then put it on the schedule. There is no task, personal or professional, that should be kept off of the schedule. This is your accountability record and the more detail that you attach, the better it will run and keep you heading in the right direction. Productivity will be yours for the taking!

- Points out areas for improvement and better ways of using your time: Assigning the right amount of time to each activity will come with time. So too will pointing out the time suckers that are robbing you of your productive time. This is a work in progress and so you will start to notice patterns and areas of improvement. That's okay and actually a healthy and helpful part of the process!

Though you may not believe that pointing out inadequacies will make you feel better, it will show you what it takes to become better at all of this. Just be honest with yourself always!

- Helps to keep you on track no matter what may come your way: When you plan out your schedule, you are going to build time in for everything. Along with that you must try your best to plan for the unforeseen. Your boss comes at you with an unexpected and urgent project -- no problem because you just have to shuffle things around on your schedule. Your child is home sick from school -- just reprioritize and utilize the daily schedule to help you to accomplish the necessities.

  You can also roll things over into your schedule for the next day as necessary, and though this is a guideline it also contains a bit of flexibility within it. This is all about productivity, and sometimes that needs to include planning for the unforeseen. Life happens, so just have a plan for it!

Carving Out and Enjoying a Bit of Me Time

"Life is what happens to you when you're busy making other plans."
-John Lennon

In our lives, we tend to make each day well planned without realizing that planning takes too much of our time as well. This quote from John Lennon, "Life is what happens to you while you're busy making other plans," has really hit home lately. Think about this and let it sink in for awhile and you will see the truth behind this quote.

I am a planner by nature, however I am learning about life these days. I am planning for new schools for the children, a new place to live, and so many other things—yet nothing is going as planned, but rather life is happening. I am seeing that I need to breathe and just enjoy "Life" because it is still happening around me!

How many times have you sat back and realized that you were so busy planning that you missed life? I have missed so many things by planning, and of course that never feels good. Don't get me wrong, I will always be a planner and world changer, but I do need to enjoy the things that happen in life even when things don't go as planned. What great and wonderful things have happened to you while you were busy making other plans? I look forward to the next year, 6 years, and 16 years of "life happening" and that's okay.

Sometimes Let Life Happen and Enjoy It

Remember that along the way in this journey of life, sometimes things won't go according to plan. If you always let a well crafted plan rule, then you will almost always get let down. I'm not saying that you shouldn't plan or get organized, clearly these things are important. Yes you need a method by which you get organized, sure you should find tools that work for you along the way, but sometimes you need to roll with it too and recognize that life is going to happen and bring in some big twists and turns.

With that being said it's absolutely essential to plan some "me time" along the way. If you don't plan for this then you are going to get burned out. If you don't allow life to happen and actually enjoy it, then you will look back with regrets. Carving time out each day and each week to do things that you enjoy is just as important as carving out time to get things done. Reward yourself, enjoy life, and by all means learn to roll with things when necessary—this doesn't mean you are unorganized but rather just realistic.

Keeping With Good Time Management Habits Moving Forward

You are in control of your destiny! Now you see that there are so many wonderful ways to get organized and to really take back your time. You can plan for your life and get organized, it just takes a bit of work along the way. Even if you have a bad day or feel particularly unproductive, it's important to just keep up with the good habits that you have learned and make them your own.

You are going to learn some things along the way and work through changes that work for YOU specifically. This is nothing to model after somebody else as this is a completely individual journey. You will make mistakes, you will have bad days, life will throw you some curve balls that you are unprepared for—but in the end having good time management and organizational skills will help you to overcome it all!

Keep It All Together and Work Towards Your Own Personal Success

It all starts to come together when you put your plan into action. When you can see that your hard work is coming together and that you make it through a day with greater productivity, then this is where the true investment into yourself pays off. Here are some guidelines and ideas to help you to keep up with your good time management skills and habits moving forward.

- Recognize that you are a work in progress and that's okay: You are not perfect, nobody is. You are going to have to work at this, and some days harder than others. You are going to learn a lot along the way and as you make mistakes you are going to learn from that. Sure sometimes all of this planning can feel rewarding and other times it will feel frustrating. Just know that for everyone it is a work in progress, and it will all come together. You will have more success than frustration, so just feel motivated and focus on the positive to keep yourself moving.

- Learn to enjoy life but know that things often won't go according to plan: Above all you need to learn to relax, which will come easier when you are organized and more productive. It sounds counterintuitive but having this structure will enable you to relax a bit and to enjoy the things that come your way. Know that sometimes you can't plan for things and that the unforeseen can happen, and be proactive in developing a strategy to work past that. Be ready to take on whatever comes your way, work at having a plan that works well for you, but do take the time to enjoy life as it comes too.

- Keep finding specific habits and tools that help you to work better: You are going to find apps that you love and then they may become a bit tired after awhile. You are going to feel tempted to try the latest organizational trend, and that's okay. Keep working at your productivity and know that this is all part of fine tuning it. If you can continue to improve upon your habits and use the right tools and methods to get you there, this means it's all working and coming together the way it's intended to. Whatever helps you to work smarter and be more productive is what it's all about in the end!

- Plan ahead and learn what it means to manage your time specifically: Creating a schedule, carving out time for each of your daily activities, and learning what it means to take charge of your day is what it's all about. Plan for the important tasks, prioritize each task, and go into each day with a sort of structure that will help you to get through it all. Manage your time, take it back, and use it to make you more productive and effective. This is going to look different for everyone, but if you can stick with it then you can really enjoy the journey much more along the way!

Conclusion

Time management is a life skill that will benefit you now and well into the long term. You have seen by now what this means and why it's so very important. You now understand what it means to be truly productive and effective, and it starts with getting organized. Life is going to always have some sort of stress, but if you can learn to stay ahead of it then it will work to your benefit.

I have given you some tips that I know to be effective, but you have to find your own plan. I understand the importance of effective time management firsthand, and it is my hope after reading this that you now do too. The more time that you invest into getting organized and being productive, the more that this will benefit you into the rest of your life. Spending the time to create a schedule and to find organizational tactics that work will help you tremendously!

Life will happen and sometimes you can't always plan for that. Just having a structure and a plan in place for the things that you do know of will help you in the long run. You CAN be a productive and efficient person, but you just have to be willing to work for it. You CAN take your time back and really get through everything you need to do in a day.

I wish you the best of luck in your journey towards productivity! You will come to appreciate and value your time, really enjoy your newfound productivity, and understand what it means to truly take your time back. Enjoy what this does for your life and the journey you experience along the way!

BONUS CHAPTER: BY JACK M. ZUFELT

This chapter is a very special gift Honorable Mr. Jack M. Zufelt

JACK ZUFELT is one of the most successful speakers and business consultants on the national and international scene.

Jack is a very popular keynote speaker. He conducts seminars and customized training programs as well as life-changing weekend retreats all over the world. His client list includes companies of all sizes including many Fortune 500 companies.

He is also the highest paid trainer in Network Marketing.

Jack's book, The DNA of Success, has catapulted him into the limelight as a celebrity business consultant, keynote speaker and trainer all around the world.

   Jack M. Zufelt
"Mentor to Millions"
Author of the #1 best-selling book,
The DNA of Success...Now in 15 Languages

Seen and heard on over 2,000 radio
and TV talk shows including The TODAY SHOW and PBS

www.TheDNAofSuccessSystem.com

To book Jack to speak at your next event go to
www.jackzufeltspeaks.com
or call his office at: 303 741-9025

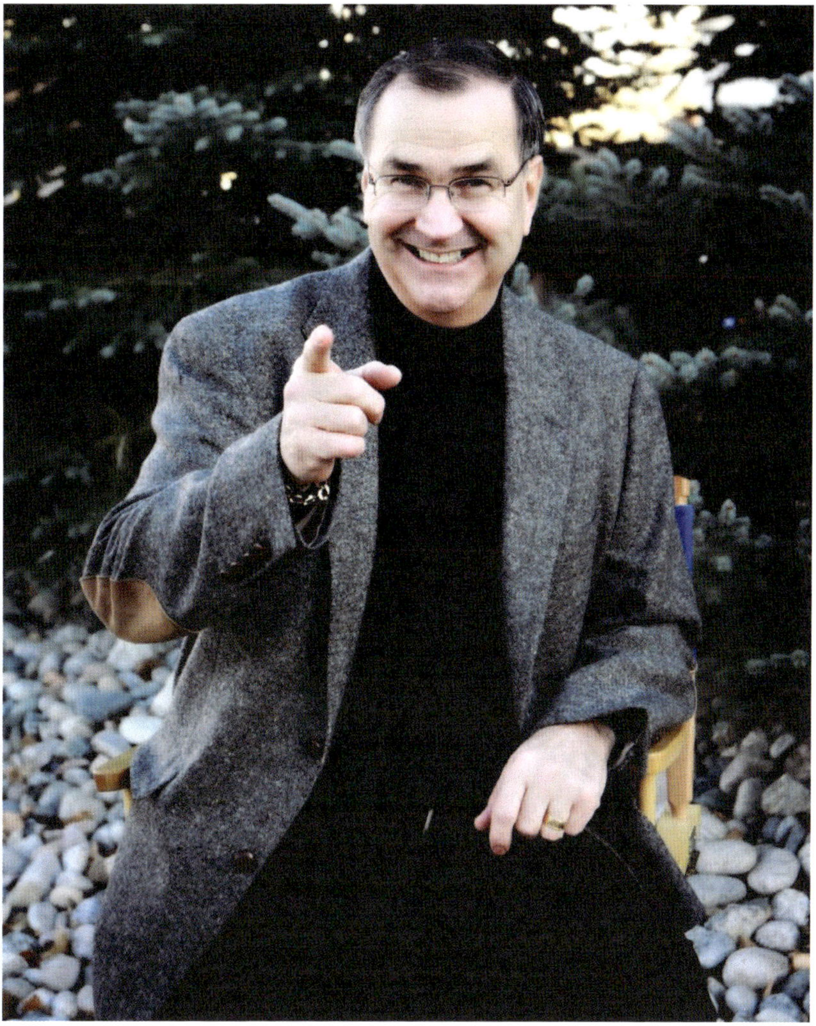

It's Easier Than You Think
By
Jack M. Zufelt

Mary, a woman about forty-two years old, had a job she did not like and was always worried about money. She was unhappy most of the time because her fifteen-year marriage was empty. They weren't at war with one another; they just weren't close or happy like they used to be. Basically they were polite roommates. Where had the happiness gone?

She loved her cat, reading, and skiing, but those things did not take away the awful feelings she had in other areas of her life. Focusing on the good and ignoring the bad did not create happiness for her any more than eating a chocolate cake with a big dose of garlic in it would make a person say mmmmm, that is good . . . if you ignore the garlic.

Pain, doubt, sorrow, anger, worry, and fear get our attention, and whatever else is going on at the time--even if it is good--will be diminished dramatically and in direct proportion to the negative emotion.

Mary was strong and capable, so she looked hard for solutions. She tried everything out there. She bought several books on how be successful in life, money, and marriage. She went to "free" motivational seminars where she heard skilled speakers whose main goal was to sell books and audio programs at the back of the room. She bought several hundred dollars worth of self-help materials with credit cards, not knowing how she was going to pay them off. She hoped these programs would show her the way out of her very deep and unhappy rut.

She faithfully wrote down her goals as she was told to do. She recited daily positive affirmations. She even carried around 3 x 5 cards with statements to be repeated throughout the day. Several times a week she would close her eyes and visualize being out of debt, owning her home free and clear, and even being slim again and happily married. She was an avid student of all these techniques, hoping they would lead her out of the parched desert to the promised land of success . . . to an oasis of happiness and plenty.

But alas, none of the techniques, tools, or tactics worked. The promised oasis always turned out to be a mirage.

At one seminar she was mesmerized by a charismatic speaker who encouraged participants to walk across hot coals barefooted. As she stepped off the hot embers to the cool ground, she thrust her hands high into the air and yelled with great enthusiasm, "I did it!" She was on a super high. She felt fabulous because, as she said it, "I faced my fear of walking on the hot coals, and I did it! If I can do that, I can do anything!" She was changed.

Or so she thought.

Once she was back home, the high she had felt diminished quickly and her life went on as usual. Nothing had changed. She was no better off than before. Her husband was still distant; she still hated her job; and she was still broke all the time.

Like far too many people, Mary was stuck. Everything she tried failed to bring her out of that hot, dry desert of dissatisfaction and despair to the promised oasis of joy, happiness and true freedom that she longed for. In fact, things were worse because she now felt bad about and doubted herself because she was not successful even after trying all those techniques. Her belief in her abilities was about as low as it could get. She began to believe that maybe she didn't have what it takes. That perhaps this was her lot in life.

To her credit she did not give up. She kept searching . . . and when she heard me speak about what it really takes to be successful, the cycle of failure stopped. Change occurred. She became free to achieve and fly high.

Millions of the people in the world experience the same thing Mary did before she found freedom. It need not be that way. You can be set free too. My main mentor, Jesus Christ, said that if you know the truth, it will set you free. I teach the truth about what it really takes to achieve joy, happiness and success….in anything and it is not what is being taught out there.

If goal setting, daily affirmations, visualization, reading self-help books, positive thinking, motivational speakers, audio programs, subliminal programming, and every other "technique" self-help gurus have sold you actually worked, then why did they not work for Mary--or you? Or the millions of people out there still seeking success?

They promise their techniques will lead you out of the desert of mediocrity or failure to the promised oasis of success. But all you get is sand in your shoes or an experience that you can add to your list of other failed attempts.

Simply stated—those techniques do not work because *they are flawed*.

The self –help movement started in the early 1900s. People achieved all kinds of *huge* success without goal setting or self-help books long before the self-help movement started. Success techniques, motivational speakers etc. did not exist before about 1935. Here are some well-known examples: The Wright brothers learned to fly without writing down goals, doing affirmations or attending motivational seminars or listen to self-help audio programs. They didn't exist. World famous inventor, Thomas Edison, did none of the things the self-help gurus purport are the only keys to success. Yet he was one of the most successful men in history.

Columbus did not come out of a seminar on real estate and decide to find a country. Same with the pharaohs who built huge pyramids! Mussolini and Hitler didn't either. You can go back in history as far as you want and you will find that people have always succeeded, sometimes despite huge barriers and obstacles.

More recent example is this: No teenager writes down on a goal list that they will get a driver's license or a car. Yet they usually get both. YOU have achieved many things that you did not write down on a goal list or read a book about or listen to a motivational speaker on how to get there. We all have.

Therefore, the ability to achieve success is *not* out there in some technique or tool or tactic. It is an inside job.

Everyone knows that we are all born with the ability to do, have, and become whatever we want. That we have the power to make things happen. And it's true! We do! That's why I call it the <u>DNA</u> of success. It IS in our DNA. I call that power within all of us the Conquering Force. It is so powerful that *nothing* stops you once it is unleashed!
Though it is with us from birth, has anyone ever taught you where the switch to this enormous power is? Nope! Not until I came along.

You have already used your Conquering Force many, many times. You got your first car and learned to drive it; learned to ski, swim, put on makeup; got a college degree; built houses; earned money--all without goal setting, affirmations, conscious daily or weekly visualization, listening to motivational speakers first, or reading books. You just went and got it because you wanted "it" with all your heart. Those were Core Desires.

Where is the switch to your Conquering Force? The answer is Core Desires. Those things you want will all your heart in any area of life. Things that are 100s on the scale of 1 to 100.

Half-hearted doesn't cut it. That is only 50 on the scale. I call these 100s Core Desires. Seventy-five on the scale isn't enough. Not even 90 is. If it is a 90 on the scale of what you want you will get 90% of the way there and stop or give up when you run into a barrier that is bigger than your desire to have that thing. Though unseen, these barriers can stop you just as a dam stops water.

Here is the problem….most people, 97%, cannot accurately identify their Core Desires, their 100s, and this is why they do not achieve at high levels. Mark Twain said this: *"I can teach anybody how to get what they want out of life. The problem is, I can't find anybody who can tell me what they want."*

Those who do know exactly what they want at 100 on the scale get them. They even seem to have extra talent or more ability than others do. Not so. Because their Conquering Force was unleashed, they acquired what was necessary to make those Core Desires a reality. More details on how to identify your Core Desires are available in my best-selling book, The DNA of Success.

Just as DNA is the chemical basis for all heredity, the DNA of success is something we all possess. This DNA of success has been with us the whole time. It is the cause of everything that anyone has ever done or will ever do. Because of it, the pyramids were built, new countries were discovered, men learned to fly and then walk on the moon. It is the cause of millions of other successes less dramatic, such as learning to drive a car, run a marathon, or shoot par golf.

Desire is THE key to ALL success. How badly do you want that thing…that end result? If it is not a 100 on the scale, a Core Desire, you will not get it because there are always obstacles and barriers that are between you and it and if those barriers are bigger than the desire…the want…that barrier will stop you permanently. And you will give up. If the desire is at 100 on the scale then you will get it.

Here are quotes by famous leaders validating the importance of desire:

"The starting point of all achievement is desire. Weak desires bring weak results just as a small fire brings a small amount of heat. When you desires are strong enough <u>you will appear to have almost super human strength</u>." **Napoleon Hill**

"It seems that intense desire creates not only its own opportunities but its own talents." **Eric Hoffer**

"Ignore what a man desires and you ignore the very source of his power." **Walter Lippman**

"<u>The first principal of success is desire</u>. If you care enough for a result, you will most certainly get it."
Robert Collier

"You must learn that whatever you are doing in life obstacles don't matter. Pain or other circumstances can be there but if you want to do a job bad enough, you'll find a way to get it done."
Jack Youngblood

"Always bear in mind that your own resolution to succeed is more important than any other thing."
 Abraham Lincoln

"A strong desire for any object will insure success for the desire of the end will point out the means."
William Hazlitt

So…you must hit the delete button and get rid of all those ideas, concepts, and methodologies on success that you have been taught and believed in for so long.

Here are five things you must delete:

1. Goal Setting. This is the granddaddy of all self-help principles, and yet it is the most damaging technique taught. How can I say that? Well, ask yourself the following questions--and be truthful:
Have you ever written down or set goals? Of course you have. Have you noticed that many, if not most, of those goals *never happened?* Millions have experienced this. It is a proven fact that eight out of ten things a person writes down on a goal list will never happen. Two will. What was there for the two that was not there for the other eight?

Goal setting not only does *not* work, but it's *negative*--even self-destructive. When you look at your list of goals and see eight out of ten of them did *not* happen, how do you feel about *you*? Thousands of people in my audiences describe how they feel like this: "I feel like a failure," "I feel bad," "I must not have what it takes," "What's wrong with me?" I never hear any positive comments. Mary certainly felt that way and almost gave up.

The two that did get done happened because they were Core Desires and that is what unleashes the Conquering Force within them so they had the determination to overcome all obstacles and barriers in the way….no matter how big they were.

2. Daily Affirmations. This one is one of the biggest frauds ever perpetrated on mankind. Have you ever recited daily affirmations like "I earn $120,000 a year" or "I am happily married" or "I am debt free" or "I weigh 120 pounds" and written them on notes you put on the bathroom mirror, refrigerator, or steering wheel of your car? How many of them became a reality? "None," most people say in my seminars.

Here is a question for you. Do you like people to lie to you? Of course not. No one does. Then why is it okay for you to lie to you? It's not. Ever! That is exactly what affirmations are. Lies. You are saying things that are not true in an attempt to convince your subconscious mind to accept them so that you will do what it takes to get what you are affirming. Trouble is, your conscious mind knows it's a lie.

By trying to turn over to your subconscious mind (which you do not control) your ability to make things happen, you actually give up control. The one thing you can and do control is your conscious mind. You can change your mind, make new decisions, learn whatever you need to learn, and even change your character and personality when you want to.

By not dealing with the truth, you will instantly and constantly be on the wrong path, and your failure is a foregone conclusion: 2 + 2 is never 5, no matter how many times you say it. The truth will, indeed, make you free. But you have to know it first. Affirmations cannot and do not make you successful.

3. Visualization. Just like affirmations, visualizing the end result you desire makes you feel good because you have been told this is a critical key to success, so you do it faithfully. Does it work? Has your income increased by $1,000 a month? Have you lost the weight? Do you have that new boat, new car, or mountain cabin you visualized? Again, the answer is always "No."

4. Self-Help Books. I ask my audiences around the world, "How many self-help books do you have?" One? Ten? Fifty? One hundred? Most admit to having between ten and fifty. One lady in my seminar in Australia said she had over 1,500! How many does it take? It takes *none!* Zero! Nada! Self-help books become "references" in your library. Dust collectors. Even my best-selling book, *The DNA of Success*, is a waste of time unless you want to know how to identify your Core Desires so that you can unleash your Conquering Force.

5. Motivational Speakers. My audiences around the globe admit that they have listened to at least one motivational speaker in person or through audio programs. I then ask, "How long did you stay motivated?" The response are always the same and unanimous . . . "2 days," "2 weeks," "till I got out of the parking lot!" "to the end of the CD." Always a very short time frame. I have concluded that motivational speakers have no lasting effect. They can make you laugh, cry, and hug everyone around you, but your life doesn't change.

This is important. When you have been successful in life, it was *not* techniques but *your* drive from within that compelled you to do, learn, and become what was needed to get the desired result.

 Back to Mary. With the advice from a friend she checked out the website of a guy who had a worldwide reputation for being boldly contrarian. His message was vastly different from all the others. A "wake up call" to the self-help industry. Warily, she listened to his conference calls. She read his book. Then, trusting once again, praying that this one would be different, she attended one of his weekend retreats.

It was as if a light came on for her. She finally knew the truth about success and achievement and why all those techniques, tools, and tactics had not worked for her. She had finally discovered the true cause of *all* achievement. She was now free from wrong and limiting paradigms. She was free from the invisible barriers that kept her from the happiness she so desperately wanted.

With this new understanding of the truth, she went on to become a very successful entrepreneur, earning enough money to live a debt-free, happy life. She lost forty pounds and was trim and in shape again! And best of all, she and her husband were close once more. The truth had set her free. That guy she learned from was me.

She had learned how to unleash her Conquering Force and that *always* results in success. In addition she learned about her invisible barriers, and with the help she got in the weekend retreat, she destroyed them. Now she was unlimited in her future.

All my successes have had *everything* to do with focusing on my Core Desires, which unleashed my Conquering Force. I did not write down a single goal or do any silly affirmations or visualizing. Motivational speakers had no lasting effect on me.

Learning how to unleash and flip the switch to the "op" position to unleash your Conquering Force, that crucial ingredient, is vital to your success--in anything. Making money, improving relationships, boosting self-esteem, gaining confidence--it all comes from the amazing Conquering Force within each of us.

Your Core Desires are the switch to your Conquering Force.

Once you know a Core Desire all you need to do is learn HOW to make it a reality. That is the easy part because it is just knowledge properly applied. Ask for help and guidance from someone who has done what you want to do, a mentor who can teach you how to get where they are because that is where you want to go too.

Your Conquering Force will destroy all obstacles including the invisible ones such as fear,   self-doubt, lack of confidence, lack of self-esteem, wrong paradigms, wrong opinions, or fear of failure. .

Now that you are aware that there is a more truthful way to achieve your heart's Core Desires, you are no longer limited. You can now become a peak performer in any area of life that matters to you. This is how everyone achieves success in anything.

Jack M. Zufelt
"Mentor to Millions"
Author of the #1 best-selling book,
The DNA of Success...Now in 15 Languages

Seen and heard on over 2,000 radio
and TV talk shows including The TODAY SHOW and PBS

www.TheDNAofSuccessSystem.com

To book Jack to speak at your next event go to
www.jackzufeltspeaks.com
or call his office at: 303 741-9025

APPENDIX SECTION

ADDITIONAL RESOURCES

Appendix: Time Management Quotes

1. "By failing to prepare, you are preparing to fail." – Benjamin Franklin
2. "Let our advance worrying become advance thinking and planning."
   -Winston Churchill
3. "Think ahead. Don't let day-to-day operations drive out planning." - Donald Rumsfeld
4. "A goal without a plan is just a wish." - Antoine de Saint-Exupéry
5. "In preparing for battle I have always found that plans are useless, but planning is indispensable." – Dwight Eisenhower
6. "I always say, don't make plans, make options." – Jennifer Aniston
7. "If you don't know where you are going, you'll end up someplace else." – Yogi Berra
8. "Never look back unless you are planning to go that way." – Henry David Thoreau

9. "Planning is bringing the future into the present so that you can do something about it now." – Alan Lakein
10. "Give me six hours to chop down a tree and I will spend the first four sharpening the axe." – Abraham Lincoln
11. "If you don't know exactly where you're going, how will you know when you get there?" – Steve Maraboli
12. "Meticulous planning will enable everything a man does to appear spontaneous." – Mark Caine
13. "Create a definite plan for carrying out your desire and begin at once, whether you are ready or not, to put this plan into action." – Napoleon Hill
14. "A good plan, violently executed now, is better than a perfect plan next week." – George Patton
15. "He who every morning plans the transaction of the day and follows out that plan, carries a thread that will guide him through the maze of the most busy life. But where no plan is laid, where the disposal of time is surrendered merely to the chance of incidence, chaos will soon reign." – Victor Hugo
16. "One reason so few of us achieve what we truly want is that we never direct our focus; we never concentrate

our power. Most people dabble their way through life, never deciding to master anything in particular." – Tony Robbins

17. "You can't depend on your eyes when your imagination is out of focus." – Mark Twain
18. "Passion is energy. Feel the power that comes from focusing on what excites you." – Oprah Winfrey
19. "Lack of direction, not lack of time, is the problem. We all have twenty-four hour days." – Zig Ziglar
20. "To conquer frustration, one must remain intensely focused on the outcome, not the obstacles." – T.F. Hodge
21. "You cannot run at full throttle when applying your mindset to all of the different things running through your head. Focusing is the key to manifesting your desires." – Stephen Richards
22. "Concentrate all your thoughts upon the work at hand. The sun's rays do not burn until brought to a focus." – Alexander Graham Bell

23. "I try to learn from the past, but I plan for the future by focusing exclusively on the present. That's where the fun is." – Donald Trump
24. "Always focus on the front windshield and not the review mirror." – Colin Powell
25. "Temperamentally anxious people can have a hard time staying motivated, period, because their intense focus on their worries distracts them from their goals." – Winifred Gallagher
26. "It's about focusing on the fight and not the fright." – Robin Roberts
27. "What do I mean by concentration? I mean focusing totally on the business at hand and commanding your body to do exactly what you want it to do." – Arnold Palmer
28. "Concentration is the secret of strength." – Ralph Waldo Emerson
29. "Inspiration is the windfall from hard work and focus. Muses are too unreliable to keep on the payroll." – Helen Hanson

30. "Once taken off one task without completing the transaction, the mind continues to seek closure. Fight to stay focused on the task at hand." – Jeff Davidson
31. "The simple act of paying positive attention to people has a great deal to do with productivity." – Tom Peters
32. "Amateurs sit and wait for inspiration, the rest of us just get up and go to work." – Stephen King
33. "If you spend too much time thinking about a thing, you'll never get it done." – Bruce Lee
34. "Stressing output is the key to improving productivity, while looking to increase activity can result in just the opposite." – Paul Gauguin
35. "Should you find yourself in a chronically leaking boat, energy devoted to changing vessels is likely to be more productive than energy devoted to patching leaks." - Warren Buffett
36. "Whenever you are asked if you can do a job, tell 'em, 'Certainly I can!' Then get busy and find out how to do it." – Theodore Roosevelt
37. "In both children and adults, there can be a hard-to-deny link between a robust sense of hope and either

work productivity or academic achievement." – Jeffrey Kluger

38. "The way we measure productivity is flawed. People checking their BlackBerry over dinner is not the measure of productivity." – Timothy Ferriss
39. "On every level of life, from housework to heights of prayer, in all judgment and efforts to get things done, hurry and impatience are sure marks of the amateur." – Evelyn Underhill
40. "The least productive people are usually the ones who are most in favor of holding meetings." – Thomas Sowell
41. "Your mind is for having ideas, not holding them." – David Allen
42. "The best time to start was last year. Failing that, today will do." – Chris Guillebeau
43. "Remember that time is money." – Benjamin Franklin
44. "There is nothing less productive than to make more efficient what should not be done at all." – Peter Drucker

45. "Start from wherever you are and with whatever you've got." – Jim Rohm
46. "Efficiency is doing things right; effectiveness is doing the right things." – Peter Drucker
47. "Just in terms of allocation of time resources, religion is not very efficient. There's a lot more I could be doing on a Sunday morning." – Bill Gates
48. "Never waste any time you can spend sleeping." – Frank Knight
49. "A particular shot or way of moving the ball can be a player's personal signature, but efficiency of performance is what wins the game for the team." – Pat Riley
50. "The higher your energy level, the more efficient your body. The more efficient your body, the better you feel and the more you will use your talent to produce outstanding results." – Tony Robbins
51. "The most efficient way to produce anything is to bring together under one management as many as possible of the activities needed to turn out the product." – Peter Drucker

52. "The first rule of any technology used in a business is that automation applied to an efficient operation will magnify the efficiency. The second is that automation applied to an inefficient operation will magnify the inefficiency." – Bill Gates
53. "The most efficient way to live reasonably is every morning to make a plan of one's day and every night to examine the results obtained." - Alexis Carrel
54. "The men who succeed are the efficient few. They are the few who have the ambition and will power to develop themselves." – Robert Burton
55. "The way to get things done is not to mind who gets the credit for doing them." – Benjamin Jowett
56. "How did it get so late so soon?" – Dr. Seuss
57. "Lost time is never found again." – Benjamin Franklin
58. "If time were to take on human form, would she be your taskmaster or freedom fighter?" – Richie Norton
59. "I like to do weird things in the shower, like drink my coffee, brush my teeth and drink a smoothie. It's good time management." – Michelle Williams

60. "Time you enjoy wasting is not wasted time." - Marthe Troly-Curtin
61. "The essence of self-discipline is to do the important thing rather than the urgent thing." – Barry Werner
62. "We are time's subjects, and time bids be gone." – William Shakespeare
63. "You can have it all. Just not all at once." – Oprah Winfrey
64. "Time is the longest distance between two places." – Tennessee Williams
65. "Procrastination is the foundation of all disasters." – Pandora Poikilos
66. "You can't make up for lost time. You can only do better in the future." – Ashley Ormon
67. "Time is what we want most, but what we spend worst." – William Penn
68. "Yesterday is gone. Tomorrow has not yet come. We have only today. Let us begin." – Mother Teresa
69. "I must govern the clock, not be governed by it." – Golda Meir

70. "The best thing about the future is that it comes one day at a time." – Abraham Lincoln
71. Yesterday is History. Tomorrow is a Mystery. –Elanor Roosevelt
72. You can't change the past, but you can ruin the present by worrying about the future. – Unknown
73. Do not dwell in the past, do not dream of the future, concentrate the mind on the present moment. – Buddha
74. The Next time you find yourself in an argument, rather than defend your position, see if you can see the other point of view first. – Richard Carlson, PH.D
75. Defer no time, delays have dangerous ends. – William Shakespeare
76. Never leave 'till tomorrow which you can do today. – Benjamin Franklin
77. He who know most grieves most for wasted time. – Dante
78. Time is what we want most, but what we use worst. – William Penn

79. The key is in not spending time. Great people think of using it. – Unknown
80. The common man is now concerned about the passage of time, the man of talent is driven by it. – Shoppenhauer
81. The Key is not spending time, but in investing it. – Stephen R. Covey
82. Time = Life; therefore, waste your time and waste your life, or master your time and master your life. –Alan Lakein
83. Don't be fooled by the calendar. There are only as many days in the year as you make use of. One man gets only a week's value out of a year while another man gets full year's value out of a week. –Charles Richards
84. Do not wait; the time will never be "just right." Start where you stand, and work with whatever tools you may have at your command, and better tools will be found as you go along. –Napoleon Hill
85. Determine never to be idle. No person will have occasion to complain of the want of time who never

loses any. It is wonderful how much can be don fi we are always doing. –Thomas Jefferson

86. Make us of time, let now advantage slip. –William Shakespeare

87. This time, like all times, is a very good one, if we but know what to do with it. –Ralph Waldo Emerson

88. A man who dares to waste one hour of life has not discovered the value of life. –Charles Darwin

89. Dost thou love life? Then do not squander time, for that is the stuff life is made of. –Benjamin Franklin

90. Never let yesterday use up today. –Richard H. Nelson

91. I don't think of the past. The only thing that matters is the everlasting present. –W. Somerset Maugham

92. It's how we spend our time here and now, that really matters. If you are fed up with way you have come up to interact with time, change it. –Marcia Wieder

93. The time for action is now. It's never too late to do something. –Carl Sandburg

94. Time and I against any two. –Baltasar Gracian

95. Time is a great healer, but poor beautician. –Lucille S. Harper

96. He that rises late must trot all day. –Benjamin Franklin
97. Yesterday is history, tomorrow is a mystery, today is a gift, that is why they call it the present. –Kung Fu Panda
98. Time stays long enough for those who use it. – Leonardo Da Vinci
99. A day wasted on others is not wasted on one's self. – Charles Dickens
100. No man goes before his time – unless the boss leaves early. –Groucho Marx
101. There is never enough time to do everything, but there is always enough time to do the most important thing. -- Brian Tracy
102. If you have two frogs, eat the ugliest one first. -- Brian Tracy
103. One of the most important rules of personal effectiveness is the 10/90 rule. -- Brian Tracy
104. You may delay, but time will not. -— Benjamin Franklin
105. Time And health are two precious assets that we don't recognize and appreciate until they have been depleted. --Denis Waitley

106. The fact is that you can't do everything that you have to do. You have to procrastinate on something. Therefore, procrastinate on small tasks. -- Brian Tracy

107. There is never enough time to do everything, but there is always enough time to do the most important thing. -- Brian Tracy

108. The purpose of time management and getting more done in less time is to enable you to spend more face time with the people you care about and doing the things that give you the greatest amount of joy in life.-- Brian Tracy.

Tips and Tricks for Handling the Stress and Time Management

• You must maintain good time management to cope with pressures, tasks, competition, whatever it may be. Determine what has to be done. This is what you must do no matter what! Consider your emotional as well as physical health -- they play a key role.

• Be real to yourself. If you do not like doing a particular task, but you know it has to be done, just do it! Or as Brian Tracy would tell you -- Just Eat the Frog!

• Take time for ALL that you need to do. You must split time for your professional and personal priorities. This approach is essential to achieving all the things you need to get done within the timeframe you have set.

• Create a budget. If you budget your money, then why not budget your time as well? Budget your time wisely though. Organizing your time wisely makes you more efficient. Trim your time down from the not so important tasks to spending more time on critical things that must be done. Counting every minute may seem stressful, but doing this actually helps alleviates the stress.

1. Make sure priorities are met. Keep a list of your main priorities each day. You must stick to this list.

2. Always schedule the most important tasks first. That way you are not getting stressed and frustrated later on.

3. Every project/task needs an action plan and sequence. Always identify the steps needed and follow that sequence.

4. Set goals that are achievable. You want to reach those goals in a reasonable amount of time.

5. Keep track of your time by synchronizing your calendars/mobile devices or just write it down.

6. Deter distractions and interruptions. No matter how big or small.

7. Expect the unexpected. Prepare for anything that may come your way.

8. Use transition time to your advantage. When you are waiting try and do something that will be beneficial or could help on an upcoming project.

9. Avoid getting overwhelmed. Do the things you're good at. Delegate other tasks.

10. Do unpleasant tasks first. Once that it out of the way you can get back to your schedule.

11. Try the 80/20 rule. This means that 20% of your effort produces 80% of your results. Think about which tasks will put you ahead of the game and let you be in control to achieve the ultimate goal.

12. Take breaks to alleviate any pressure.

13. Try Yoga or Meditation. These are great stress relievers.

14. Be lenient to yourself. Don't beat yourself up if everything does not go the right way at the same time. You have to have some flexibility and the mindset to keep moving forward. You do not have to be right all the time.

15. Say no. You cannot please everyone and do everything that is asked. Do what you feel comfortable doing and stick to it.

16. Outsource. Things that are taking up too much time should be given to someone else. If you really do not like doing something or feel someone else is more qualified then pass that task along. If it can be done faster, better and cheaper then definitely outsource.

17. Time Management vs. Health Management. Bad health could be a sign of bad time management. Constantly being late or not completing tasks on time and to the best of your ability will lead to stress and health problems.

18. Lose the negativity. Do not think negative thoughts or doubt your own self-worth or surround yourself with negative people.

19. Time Value = Opportunity Value. Do it now. Take the opportunity that is given to you as you may not have that opportunity again.

20. Remain focused. Be very specific and true to yourself. It is all in the details and thoughts that you plan in your time management schedule.

21. Visualize calmness. Picture serenity and tranquility.

22. Have a mantra. A positive statement that helps with your coping ability.

23. Write notes to yourself. You will see things clearly and better because they are written down.

24. Collect yourself. If you are in a stressful situation, count to 10 or 20. Relax and unwind.

25. Smell the roses or tulips. Try Aromatherapy oils. They are therapeutic to the mind and soul. Basil, Chamomile, Eucalyptus, Lavender, Peppermint, Rose and Thyme are known for their calming and soothing effects.

26. Try tea or a healthy snack. Instead of drinking alcohol, try green tea or chamomile tea or whatever tea you like. Eating nuts and raw fruits and vegetables is beneficial and a great stress reliever, plus it is healthier than eating salty potato chips.

27. Sit up straight. Slumping causes breathing problems and back problems.

28. Stand up. Do not sit for hours on end or even one hour. Try standing up every 15 minutes if you can, if only for a few minutes. Walk to another room or walk to window and look out.

29. Stretch. When you stretch you loosen muscles that become stiff.

30. Get some sun. At least 15 or 20 minutes a day can help significantly reduce stress.

31. Focus on your time. What is most valuable to you? Organize your time, tasks and abilities to be more productive.

32. Keep others in the loop. Let everyone around you know what is important and necessary to achieve the goals that are set.

33. Make a chart. Show everyone the progress for each project and task so they will know what is being completed and what remains to be done.

34. Mission Possible. Vision Critical. Keep with the mission and vision that is set forth. Think out the details for the mission and visualize the outcome when complete.

35. Be professional at all times. Always keep your cool when dealing with others whether they are clients or customers or employees. Show respect towards others and they will respect you. Being professional and courteous will ensure others will always want to do business with you.

36. Speed-Read. Even if you have to take a course this is a very important skill to help you make it through so much information that is thrown your way. You will gain higher levels of both retention and comprehension.

37. Brain-Storm. Develop creative thinking with employees. Listen to all ideas and come to an agreement on the good ones.

38. Add value to your thinking. Don't just think about what to do next, think about what has already been done. Did it work out from the beginning or did you have to continuously tweak

and tinker to get it done successfully, which caused you to waste valuable time.

39. Constantly balance your home life and work life. Staying stress and worry free at work will enable you to be a happier person outside work. Don't always take work home, but on the other hand do not bring your problems at home to work.

40. Identify what limits you. Is it financial constraints, is the market, is it production, perhaps it's the competition. You should focus on this and get a hold of it to boosts sales.

Managing Your Stress

1. Do You Truly Understand Stress? Can you tell when you are stressed? What can you do to cope with stress?

2. Find out the True Cause of Your Stress. Is it work- related, relationship, family, financial, health? Maybe something bothering you from your past.

3. Know Your Stress Warnings. Do the slightest distractions or noises easily irritate you? Are you having problems concentrating? Are you constantly feeling angry or upset at the littlest things? Do you regularly get headaches? Do you feel lackluster?

4. Determine How You Cope With Stress. Are you binge/over eating? Do you drink and drink and drink thinking it is helping you in some way? Does the stress come in go in certain situations or is it constantly nagging you?

5. Are You Finding Healthy Ways to Deal With Stress? Meditation or yoga or deep breathing techniques are great at relieving stress and making you feel better. Eat the proper foods, get plenty of sleep, try exercising, take breaks and vacations. Seeking support from family and friends can also be beneficial.

Time Wasters That Are Stressful

1. Constantly on the Telephone /Cell Phone
2. Lack of Self-Discipline
3. Management by Crisis
4. Ineffective Delegation
5. Paperwork Overload
6. Socializing
7. Worrying
8. Facebook, Twitter, Instagram
9. Smoking
10. Drinking in Excess
11. Waiting
12. Procrastination
13. Disorganization
14. Television
15. Internet Surfing
16. Playing Video/Online Games
17. Instant Messaging
18. Over-Reliance on Email
19. Ineffective Multi-Tasking
20. Cluttered Work Area

You must maintain good time management to cope with pressures, tasks, competition, whatever it may be. Determine what has to be done. This is what you must do no matter what! Consider your emotional as well as physical health -- they play a key role.

• Be real to yourself. If you do not like doing a particular task, but you know it has to be done, just do it! Or as Brian Tracy would tell you -- Just Eat the Frog!

• Take time for ALL that you need to do. You must split time for your professional and personal priorities. This approach is essential to achieving all the things you need to get done within the timeframe you have set.

• Create a budget. If you budget your money, then why not budget your time as well? Budget your time wisely though. Organizing your time wisely makes you more efficient. Trim your time down from the not so important tasks to spending more time on critical things that must be done. Counting every minute may seem stressful, but doing this actually helps alleviates the stress.

1. Keep a list of your main priorities each day.   You must stick to this list.

2. Always schedule the most important tasks first. That way you are not getting stressed and frustrated later on.

3. Every project/task needs an action plan and sequence. Always identify the steps needed and follow that sequence.

4. Set goals that are achievable. You want to reach those goals in a reasonable amount of time.

5. Keep track of your time by synchronizing your calendars/mobile devices or just write it down.

6. Deter distractions and interruptions. No matter how big or small.

7. Expect the unexpected. Prepare for anything that may come your way.

8. Use transition time to your advantage. When you are waiting try and do something that will be beneficial or could help on an upcoming project.

9. Avoid getting overwhelmed. Do the things you're good at. Delegate other tasks.

10. Do unpleasant tasks first. Once that it out of the way you can get back to your schedule.

11. Try the 80/20 rule. This means that 20% of your effort produces 80% of your results. Think about which tasks will put you ahead of the game and let you be in control to achieve the ultimate goal.

12. Take breaks to alleviate any pressure.

13. Try Yoga or Meditation. These are great stress relievers.

14. Be lenient to yourself. Don't beat yourself up if everything does not go the right way at the same time. You have to have some flexibility and the mindset to keep moving forward. You do not have to be right all the time.

15. Say no. You cannot please everyone and do everything that is asked. Do what you feel comfortable doing and stick to it.

16. Outsource. Things that are taking up too much time should be given to someone else. If you really do not like doing something or feel someone else is more qualified then pass that task along. If it can be done faster, better and cheaper then definitely outsource.

17. Time Management vs. Health Management. Bad health could be a sign of bad time management. Constantly being late or not completing tasks on time and to the best of your ability will lead to stress and health problems.

18. Lose the negativity. Do not think negative thoughts or doubt your own self-worth or surround yourself with negative people.

19. Time Value = Opportunity Value. Do it now. Take the opportunity that is given to you as you may not have that opportunity again.

20. Be very specific and true to yourself. It is all in the details and thoughts that you plan in your time management schedule.

Breathing and Yoga Techniques for Stress Management

(Illustrated by Tameisha Shevelle Harrington)

Legal Disclaimer

This book is not intended to treat, diagnose or prescribe. Author, Publishers, Editors, and all other contributors have provided this material for entirely educational purposes. Use(s) of this information is entirely the responsibility of those who choose to apply this information for their personal health and wellbeing. This information is not intended as prescription, prognosis or diagnosis for any disease or illness, and should not be used as a replacement for any medical treatment you may currently be undergoing. It is not intended to substitute the medical expertise and advice of your primary health care provider. We encourage you to discuss any decisions about treatment or care with your health care provider.

The mention of any product, service, or therapy is not an endorsement by the publisher and its affiliates. The information provided is solely the opinion of the individual(s) and is, again, for educational purposes only. Application of information provided without supervision of a licensed medical doctor is done so at the individuals own risk.

Breathing Techniques (Pranayam) (Pranayam)

Method 1 of 6: Bhastrika Pranayam: Bellows Breath

Breathe in deeply through your nostrils. First, feel the diaphragm move down, allowing the lungs to expand and forcing the abdomen out; then feel your chest expand with your collar bones rising last.

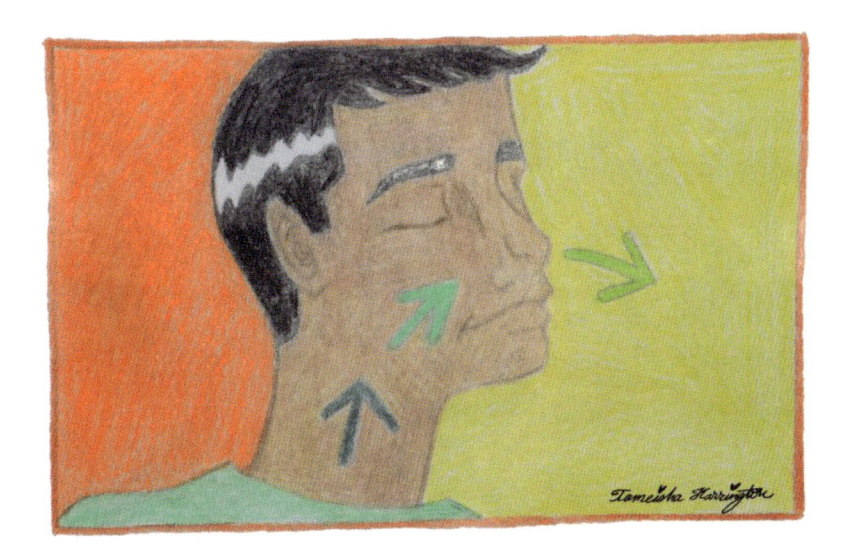

Breath out quickly through your nostrils. Feel the collar bones dropping, chest deflating, and abdomen shrinking as the lungs collapse. This process of exhaling should be much faster than the process of inhaling -- almost like a rapid deflation.

Repeat the process. When correctly done, your chest will expand when you breathe in and deflate when you breathe out. Continue doing this for 5 minutes.

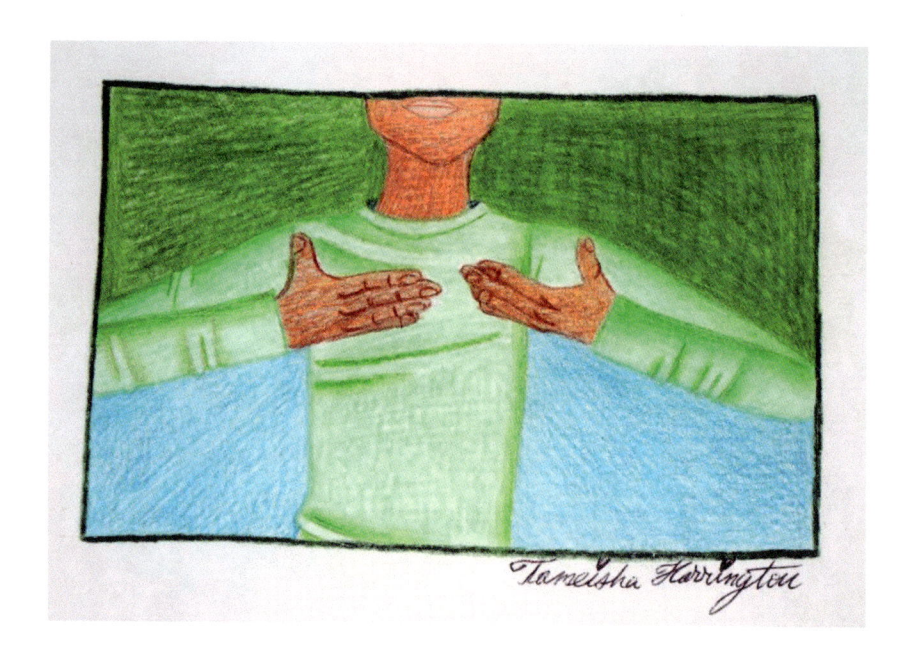

With practice, speed up your breathing. Beginners should always start slowly to avoid hyperventilating, but over time, it will be possible to turn this into a rapid breathing technique.

Method 2 of 6: Kapalbhati Pranayam: Shining Forehead Breath

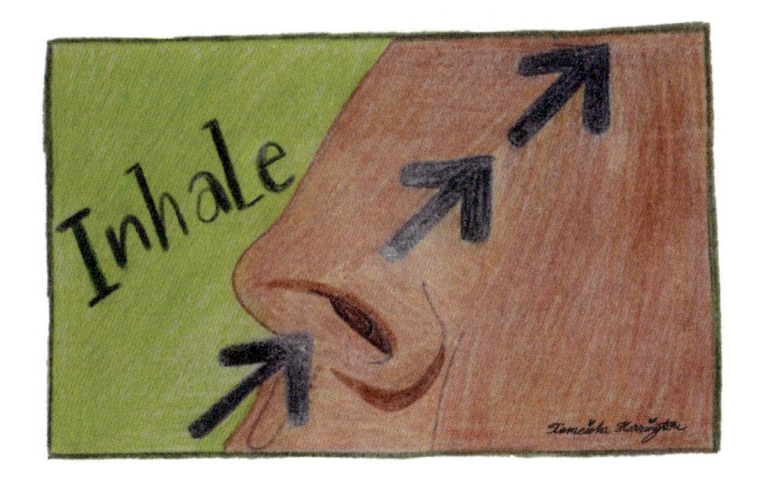

Exhale through both nostrils forcefully. This places the emphasis of the breath on the exhale rather than the (natural) inhale. Assist your exhalation by pulling in your stomach muscles to expel air. Exhaling should take much less time than it took to inhale.

"Forced" exhalation means that the contraction of your stomach muscles helps push the air out of your body. It does not mean that the exhalation should be uncomfortable for you in any way.

Repeat breaths for 15 minutes. You may take a minute's rest after every five minutes.

Method 3 of 6: Anulom Vilom Pranayam: Alternate Nostril Breath

1-Close your eyes. Focus your attention on your breathing.

2-Close the right nostril with the right thumb. Simply press the thumb against your nostril to block it.

3-Inhale slowly through the left nostril. Fill your lungs with air. First, feel the diaphragm move down, allowing the lungs to expand and forcing the abdomen out; then feel your chest expand with your collar bones rising last.

4-Remove your thumb from your right nostril. Keep your right hand by your nose and your lungs full of air.

5-Use your ring and middle finger to close your left nostril. Most people find it easier to continue using the same hand to block either nostril, but you're welcome to switch hands depending on which nostril you're blocking.
You can also switch if your arm gets tired.

6-Exhale slowly and completely with the right nostril. Feel the collar bones dropping, chest deflating, and abdomen shrinking as the lungs collapse. When you've finished exhaling, keep your left nostril closed.

7-Inhale through the right nostril. Fill your lungs.

8-Close the right nostril and open the left.

9-Breathe out slowly through the left nostril. This process is one round of Anulom Vilom Pranayam.

10-Continue for 15 minutes. You may take a minute's rest after every five minutes of exercise.

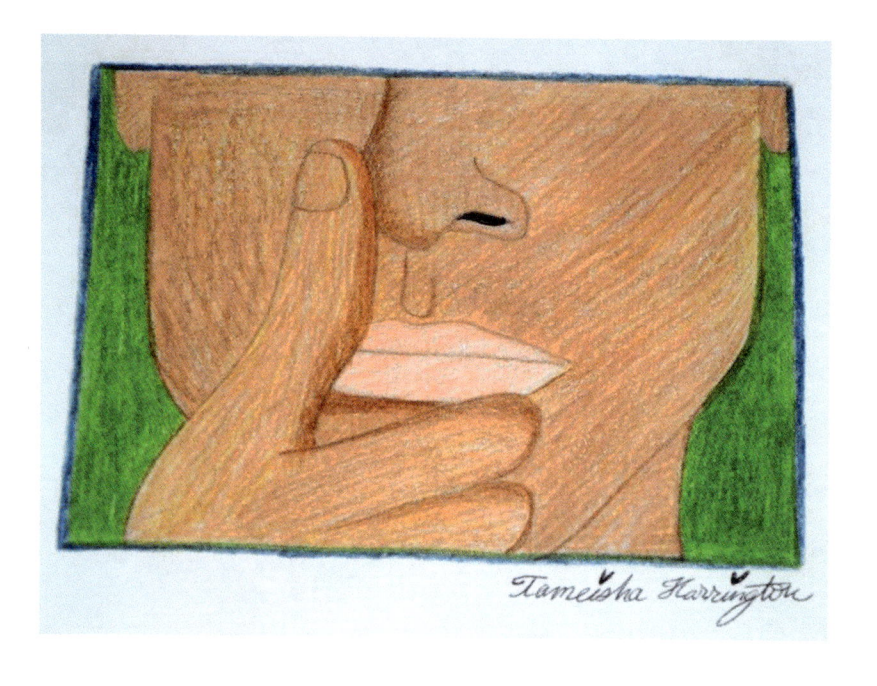

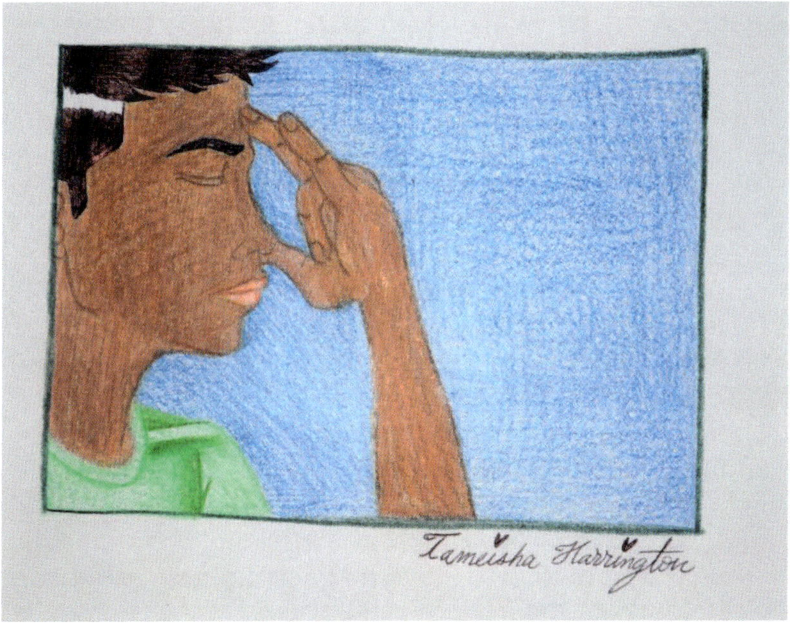
Tameisha Harrington

Method 4 of 6: Bahya Pranayam: External Breath

1-Inhale deeply through your nose. First, feel the diaphragm move down, allowing the lungs to expand and forcing the abdomen out; then feel your chest expand with your collar bones rising last.

2-Exhale forcefully. Use your stomach and diaphragm to push the air from your body. "Forced" exhalation means that the contraction of your stomach muscles helps push the air out of your body. It does not mean that the exhalation should be uncomfortable for you in any way.

3-Touch your chin to your chest and suck in your stomach completely. The goal is to leave a hollow below your ribcage, making it look like the front muscle wall of your abdomen is pressed against the back. Hold this position -- and your breath -- for as long as is comfortable.

4-Lift your chin and breathe in slowly. Allow your lungs to completely fill with air.

5-Repeat 3 to 5 times.

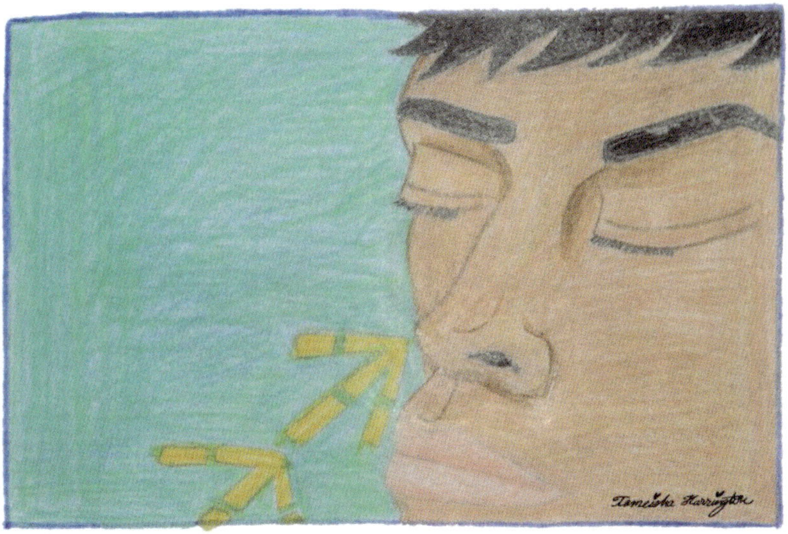

Method 5 of 6: Bhramari Pranayam: Bee Breath

1-Close your eyes. Focus on your breathing.

2-Place your thumbs in your ears, your index fingers above your eyebrows, and your remaining along the sides of your nose. Keep each pinky finger near a nostril.

3-Breath in deeply through the nose. First, feel the diaphragm move down, allowing the lungs to expand and forcing the abdomen out; then feel your chest expand with your collar bones rising last.

4-Use your pinkies to partially close each nostril. Keep your lungs filled.

5-Breathe out through the nose while humming. Note that the humming sound should originate in your throat, not as a result of your partially-blocked nostrils.

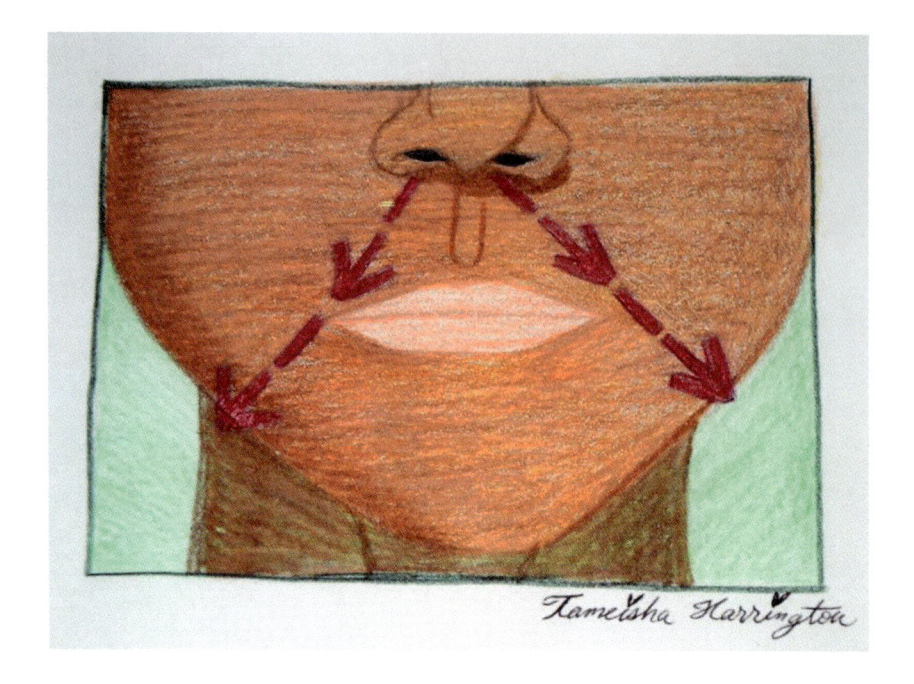

6-Repeat three times.

Method 6 of 6: Udgeeth Pranayam: Chanting Breath

Yoga poses found to be helpful in calming the brain and reducing the stress and anxiety

Pose: Paschimottanasana_SEATED FORWARD BEND

Pose: Dolphin Pose_DOLPHIN POSE

Pose: Cow-Pose

Bitilasana (Cow Pose)

Pose: Marjaryasana_CAT POSE

Pose: Ustrasana_CAMEL POSE

Ustrasana (Camel Pose)

Pose: Bhujangasana_COBRA POSE

Pose: Bharadvajasana Twist

Pose: Dandasana_STAFF POSE

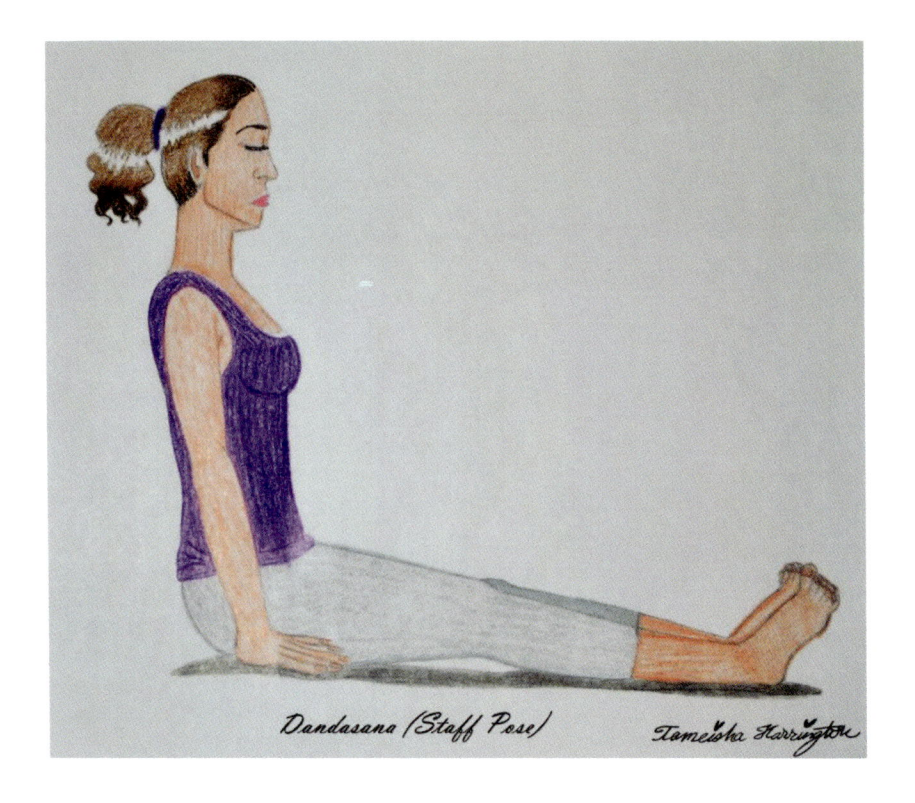

Pose: Dolphin Plank Pose

Pose: Balasana_CHILDS POSE

Pose: Uttanasana - STANDING FORWARD BEND

Pose: Setu Bandha Sarvangasana - BRIDGE POSE

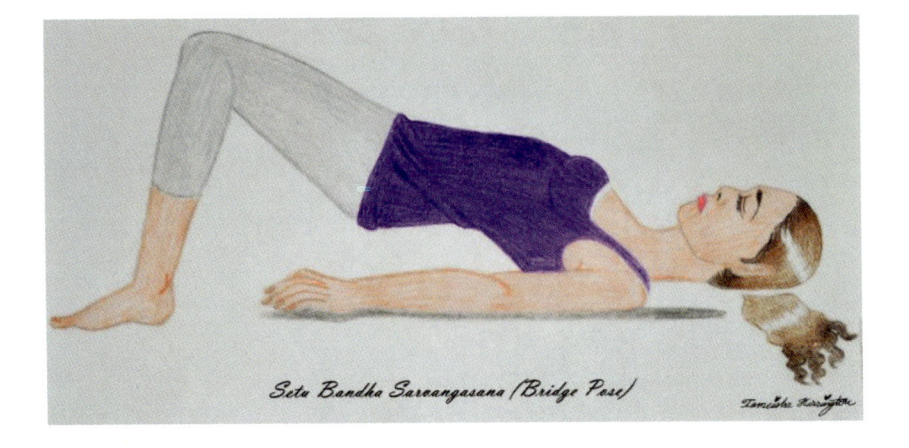

Pose: Utthita Trikonasana - EXTENDED TRIANGLE POSE

Pose: Parivrtta Janu Sirsasana - REVOLVED HEAD TO KNEE POSE

Pose: Dhanurasana - BOW POSE

Dhanurasana (Bow Pose)

Pose: Matsyasana - FISH POSE

Matsyasana (Fish Pose) — Tameisha Harrington

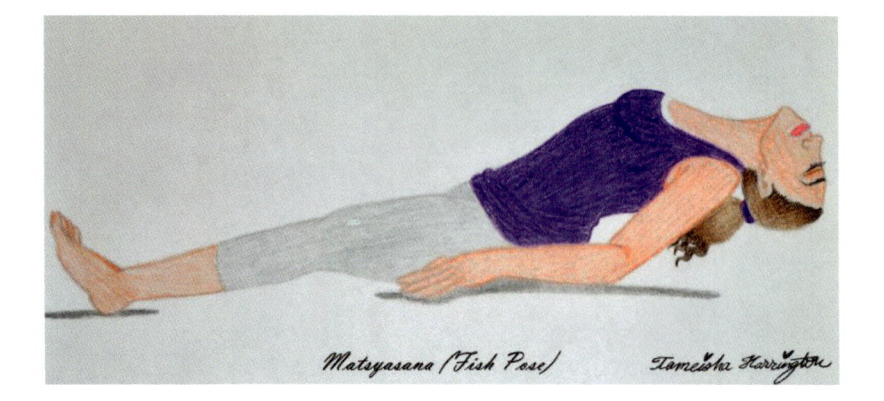

Pose: Anjali Mudra - SALUTATION SEAL

Pose: Sukhasana - EASY POSE

Pose: Savasana - CORPSE POSE

About Tameisha Shevelle Harrington:

Tameisha Shevelle Harrington was born and raised in St. Louis, MO. She has loved art and in particular drawing since she was a young girl. She became a member of the YAP (Young Artist Program) at Craft Alliance in University City, where she developed her skills and learned various teachings of art ranging from drawing, cartooning, painting, ceramics, glass bead making and realism. Tameisha has a self portrait mural along with the other Young Artist on the front of the Craft Alliance building. During her senior year at Kirkwood Senior High School she was one of the first art students for the newly created AP Studio Art Class in 2007. She learned a great deal in this class and really knew by then she wanted her career to involve art. Even though her classes taught her a lot about art she has self taught herself as well. She is very detailed and dedicated to creating the kind of art that is colorful and fun.

You can view Tameisha's art online at Shevelle Creations on Facebook, **MySLART.org**, and also art for sale on *Artwanted.com*.

Appendix: Outsourcing Resources

Why Outsource?

Outsourcing helps save you time in the long run. After all, that is what this book is all about. If you do not have the resources in your company and you need to get a project completed then outsourcing to the right person can set your mind at ease. By outsourcing to one person or three different individuals to get small projects and research done will free up your time to manage and focus more on the core items. You are not taking on another employee full-time or even part-time which will save money as well. You want to make sure you know what you are getting in return. Check around and make sure the person is well qualified and experienced in what it is you are depending on them to do. Let them know exactly what it is you need completed and if there is a specific time frame in which the project or task needs to be finished and back to you.

What are the true benefits of outsourcing?

- Better Services
- Less Expensive
- Faster Productivity

- Better Services
- Reduced Capital
- Efficiency
- Productivity
- Market Presence

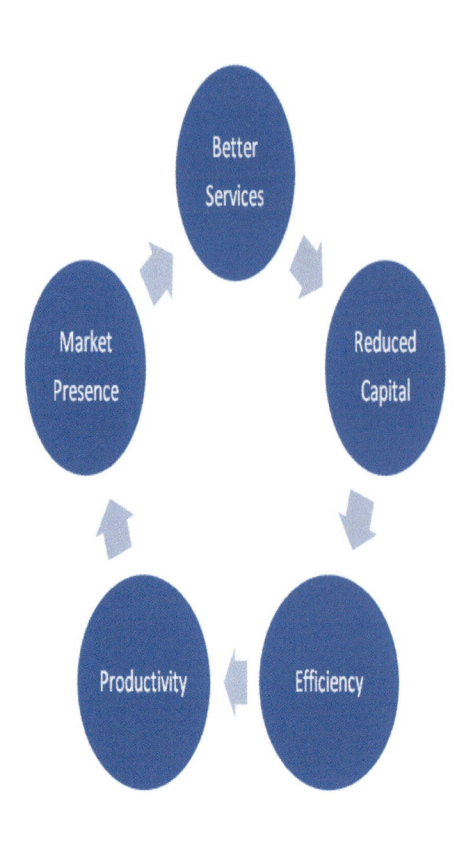

Outsourcing is used by big companies as well as small companies or even individuals. These days, a lot of companies use overseas sources and development teams that complete tasks and jobs to deliver quality products or services. You want to have a great contact list of qualified and dependable people that can get the job done in an efficient, satisfactorily and timely manner.

You know you cannot possibly get everything done by yourself. Whether you need flyers, a new website, videos created, a marketing campaign or whatever the project may be you want to find someone who is good at that particular job.

1. Focus

If you can outsource certain tasks then you can focus on your specific challenges and goals for the company. You would be able to avoid distractions that may pop up if you need to research and find something on the internet by simply giving the job to your outsource specialist with the full understanding that they will have the information to you at a certain time and within budget.

2. Time efficiency

Find one person to do one thing and another to do something totally different. With each person doing their own thing, the specialist can get it done at a greater speed, with better dexterity and productivity.

3. Cost

While you cannot complete all of the tasks that need to be done by yourself, you can have a small team of outsourced individuals to call upon when needed. This will save you time, money and headaches because you are able to focus on other more important tasks and new endeavors that may come up.

Your ultimate goal is to save money and have a much needed project completed when you want it.

4. Expertise

We have certain skills that we are good at and others, well not so much. When you find a dependable individual(s) with whom you can rely on for their knowledge and expertise then you need to keep them close. While you may have to vision for a new idea or project, someone else can provide the know how to bring it to life efficiently and effectively.

5. Market Knowledge

If you have an outsourced guru who is in the know with all the latest trends and regulations that is a critical factor in enabling your business to succeed. They will know where to get valuable information and keep you up-to-date to develop the kind of business you envisioned.

6. Overhead

This is relatively plain and simple. Yes you will need key employees on a daily basis to help with your business, but you do not need or want to hire to many workers as this will drive your overhead costs up. Not only that, but they would require hardware and equipment, desks, computers, training, telephones, etc…
With outsourcing all you will need is to call or e-mail the individual(s) and let them know exactly what you need and when.

7. Multi-platform

When there is growth in new segments, it is beneficial that your growth expands through multi-channels and multi-platforms. Being able to outsource to specialist with this niche can help grow and spread your business to new audiences.

8. Scope

While we have learned valuable skills in specific tasks over time, it is a must that we have others around us who can help with the broader scope of things: everything from start-up to product creation to design to development to marketing. If we limit ourselves to only working with certain knowledge and skills that we have, trying to expand and grow the business can be limited and restricted. We may miss out on new discoveries and developments in our fields. By combining our skills and working with our go-to specialists who are more knowledgeable and current on what is going on in the marketplace the scope of the business can steadily grow and increase revenue.

Appendix: Outsourcing Resources

Website Title	Website URL LINK
BPOVIA | Award-winning Virtual Assistant Service Provider - BPOVIA Virtual Assistant and Knowledge Process Outsourcing Service	bpovia.com

BPOVIA

Select Language:

Home | Service | Plans & Pricing | Success Stories | Contact Us | FAQs | Testimonials | Affiliate | Blog

Live Service Request from Clients Worldwide.

Live Client Task
- Client from Whippany submitted Cartoon Making task
- Client from Plymouth submitted Research task
- Client from Montana submitted Office Administrative task
- Client from Nebraska submitted Website Maintenance task

Visitor from is browsing BPOVIA website

What Do You Need Done?
- iPhone & Android Development
- Design & Multimedia

What Our Clients Love About BPOVIA
Want to know why more than 10,000 professionals, entrepreneurs, small & medium sized business all around world choose BPOVIA?

Website Title	Website URL LINK
Whichlance | Comparison site of Outsourcing, Crowdsourcing and Freelance web sites	whichlance.com

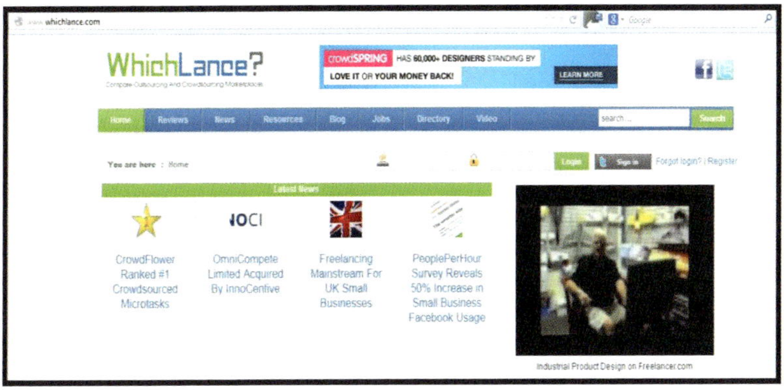
whichlance.com
WhichLance?
crowdSPRING HAS 60,000+ DESIGNERS STANDING BY
LOVE IT OR YOUR MONEY BACK!
LEARN MORE
Home
Reviews
News
Resources
Blog
Jobs
Directory
Video
search ...
Search
You are here : Home
Login
Sign in
Forgot login? | Register
Latest News
CrowdFlower Ranked #1 Crowdsourced Microtasks
OmniCompete Limited Acquired By InnoCentive
Freelancing Mainstream For UK Small Businesses
PeoplePerHour Survey Reveals 50% Increase in Small Business Facebook Usage
Industrial Product Design on Freelancer.com

Website Title	Website URL LINK
Advice | French Market Place	avdice.com

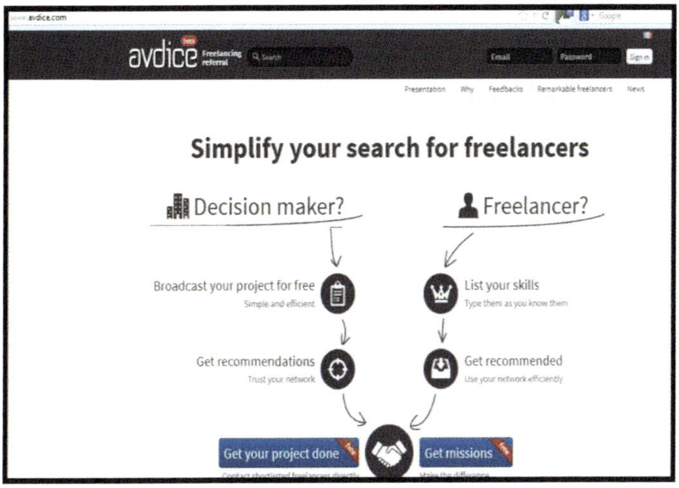
avdice.com
avdice
beta
Freelancing referral
Search
Email
Password
Sign in
Presentation
Why
Feedbacks
Remarkable freelancers
News
Simplify your search for freelancers
Decision maker?
Freelancer?
Broadcast your project for free
Simple and efficient
List your skills
Type them as you know them
Get recommendations
Trust your network
Get recommended
Use your network efficiently
Get your project done
free
Get missions
free

Website Title	Website URL LINK
Whizzat | is a web-platform that connects experts	whizzat.com

whizzat

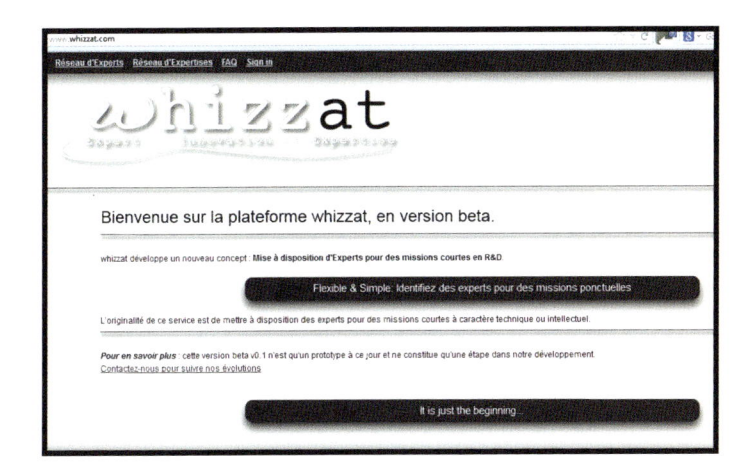

Réseau d'Experts | Réseau d'Expertises | FAQ | Sign in

Bienvenue sur la plateforme whizzat, en version beta.

whizzat développe un nouveau concept : **Mise à disposition d'Experts pour des missions courtes en R&D.**

Flexible & Simple: Identifiez des experts pour des missions ponctuelles

L'originalité de ce service est de mettre à disposition des experts pour des missions courtes à caractère technique ou intellectuel.

Pour en savoir plus : cette version beta v0.1 n'est qu'un prototype à ce jour et ne constitue qu'une étape dans notre développement. Contactez-nous pour suivre nos évolutions.

It is just the beginning

Website Title	**Website URL LINK**
Science Exchange | online CtoC marketplace for outsourcing scientific experiments, from academic scientists to academic scientists (StoS).	**scienceexchange.com**

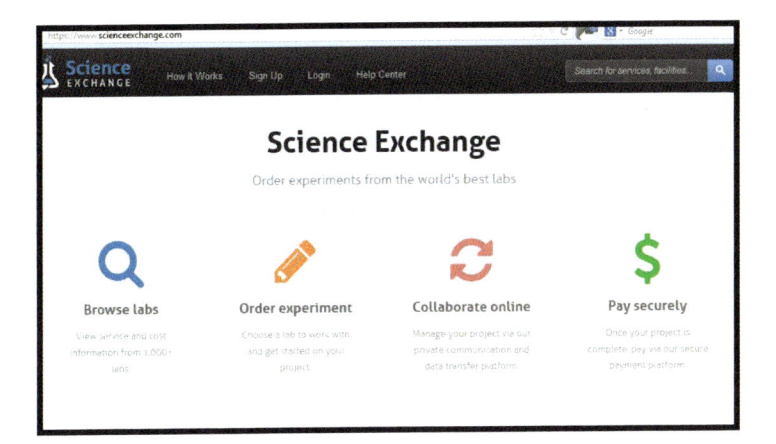

Science Exchange

Order experiments from the world's best labs

Browse labs
View service and cost information from 1,000+ labs

Order experiment
Choose a lab to work with and get started on your project

Collaborate online
Manage your project via our private communication and data transfer platform

Pay securely
Once your project is complete, pay via our secure payment platform

Website Title	Website URL LINK
**Zintro	you can find a consultant, expert, or industry specialist for quick phone consultations or longer engagements**	zintro.com

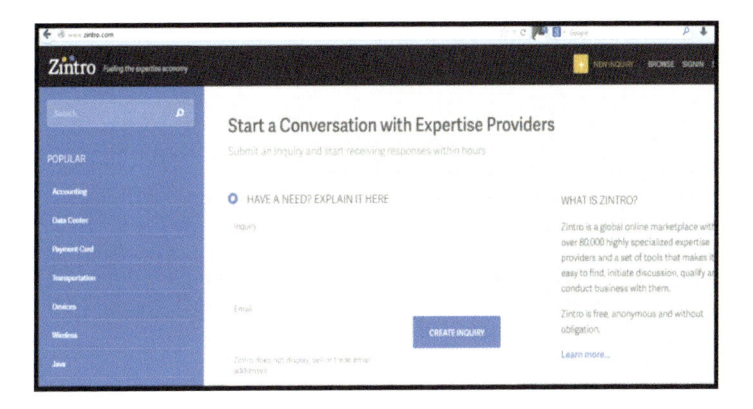

Website Title	Website URL LINK
Peopleperhour | marketplace allowing businesses to find, hire and manage freelancers remotely all over the world.	peopleperhour.com

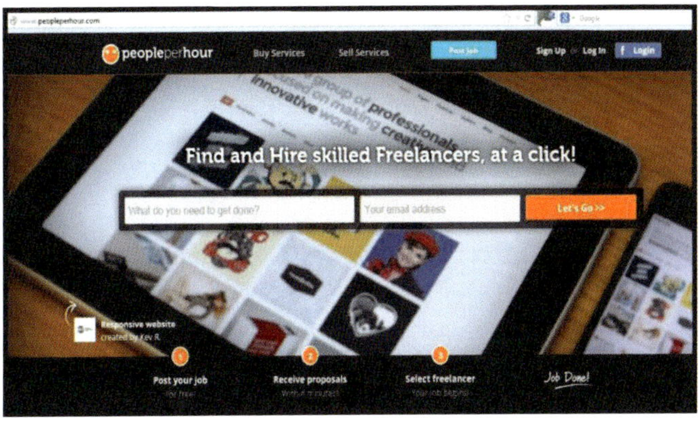
www.peopleperhour.com
peopleperhour
Buy Services
Sell Services
Post Job
Sign Up
Log In
Login
Find and Hire skilled Freelancers, at a click!
What do you need to get done?
Your email address
Let's Go >>
Responsive website
Post your job
Receive proposals
Select freelancer
Job Done!

Website Title	Website URL LINK
**Freelancer	you can find expert programmers, designers, writers, translators, marketers, researchers and admin contractors**	**freelancer.com**

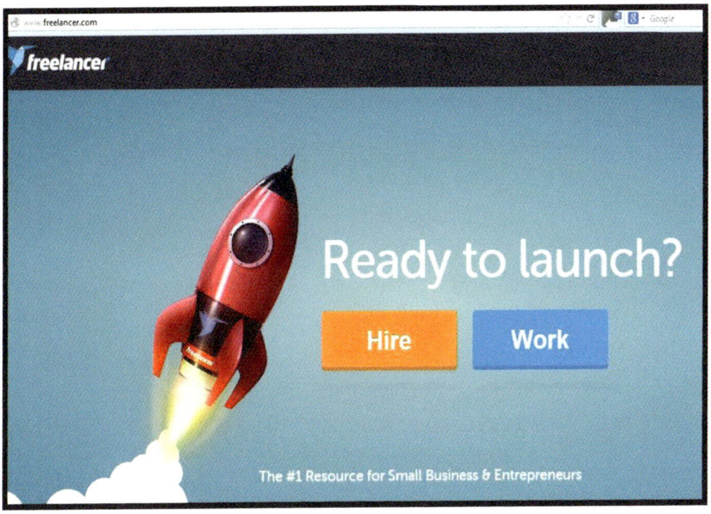
www.freelancer.com
freelancer
Ready to launch?
Hire
Work
The #1 Resource for Small Business & Entrepreneurs

Website Title	Website URL LINK
Elance | you can find expert programmers, designers, writers, translators, marketers, researchers and admin contractors	elance.com

Find Freelancers
Find Work
Talent Clouds
How it Works
Sign In
Elance
work differently
Browse Categories
Search Freelancers
Go
Hire Great Freelancers
DANIEL B.
Video/Animator
"I work with really talented clients from around the world." »
Post Your Job (it's free)
Hiring? Find amazing freelancers online.
Register Now (it's free)

Website Title	Website URL LINK
Source Experts | an outsourcing network for companies and freelancers	sourceexperts.com

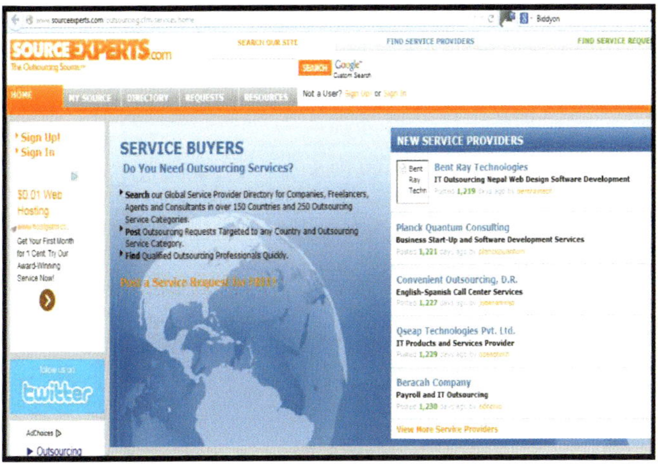
SOURCEEXPERTS.com
SEARCH OUR SITE
FIND SERVICE PROVIDERS
SEARCH
Google Custom Search
HOME
MY SOURCE
DIRECTORY
REQUESTS
RESOURCES
Not a User?
Sign Up!
Sign In
$0.01 Web Hosting
Get Your First Month for 1 Cent. Try Our Award-Winning Service Now!
twitter
AdChoices
Outsourcing
SERVICE BUYERS
Do You Need Outsourcing Services?
Search our Global Service Provider Directory for Companies, Freelancers, Agents and Consultants in over 150 Countries and 250 Outsourcing Service Categories.
Post Outsourcing Requests Targeted to any Country and Outsourcing Service Category.
Find Qualified Outsourcing Professionals Quickly.
NEW SERVICE PROVIDERS
Bent Ray Technologies
IT Outsourcing Nepal Web Design Software Development
Planck Quantum Consulting
Business Start-Up and Software Development Services
Convenient Outsourcing, D.R.
English-Spanish Call Center Services
Qseap Technologies Pvt. Ltd.
IT Products and Services Provider
Beracah Company
Payroll and IT Outsourcing
View More Service Providers

Website Title	Website URL LINK
1000consultants | an online media dedicated to IT-web industry. Consultants and companies can also publish their CV and job offers.	1000consultants.com

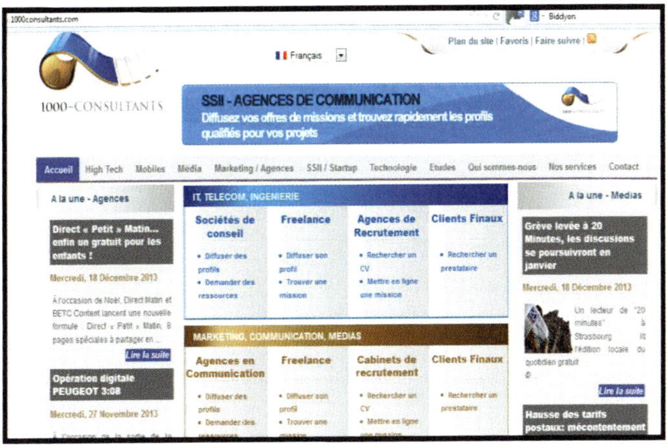
1000consultants.com
Plan du site | Favoris | Faire suivre |
Français
1000-CONSULTANTS
SSII - AGENCES DE COMMUNICATION
Diffusez vos offres de missions et trouvez rapidement les profils qualifiés pour vos projets
Accueil
High Tech
Mobiles
Média
Marketing / Agences
SSII / Startup
Technologie
Etudes
Qui sommes-nous
Nos services
Contact
A la une - Agences
Direct « Petit » Matin... enfin un gratuit pour les enfants !
Mercredi, 18 Décembre 2013
A l'occasion de Noël, Direct Matin et BETC Content lancent une nouvelle formule « Direct « Petit » Matin, 8 pages spéciales à partager en ...
Lire la suite
Opération digitale PEUGEOT 3:08
Mercredi, 27 Novembre 2013
IT, TELECOM, INGENIERIE
Sociétés de conseil
Diffuser des profils
Demander des ressources
Freelance
Diffuser son profil
Trouver une mission
Agences de Recrutement
Rechercher un CV
Mettre en ligne une mission
Clients Finaux
Rechercher un prestataire
MARKETING, COMMUNICATION, MEDIAS
Agences en Communication
Diffuser des profils
Demander des ressources
Freelance
Diffuser son profil
Trouver une mission
Cabinets de recrutement
Rechercher un CV
Mettre en ligne une mission
Clients Finaux
Rechercher un prestataire
A la une - Medias
Grève levée à 20 Minutes, les discusions se poursuivront en janvier
Mercredi, 18 Décembre 2013
Un lecteur de "20 minutes" à Strasbourg lit l'édition locale du quotidien gratuit
Lire la suite
Hausse des tarifs postaux: mécontentement

Website Title	Website URL LINK
**P2people	innovative micro outsourcing service that makes it easy for people, freelancers and businesses to outsource their jobs and freelance their services**	p2people.co.uk

p2people

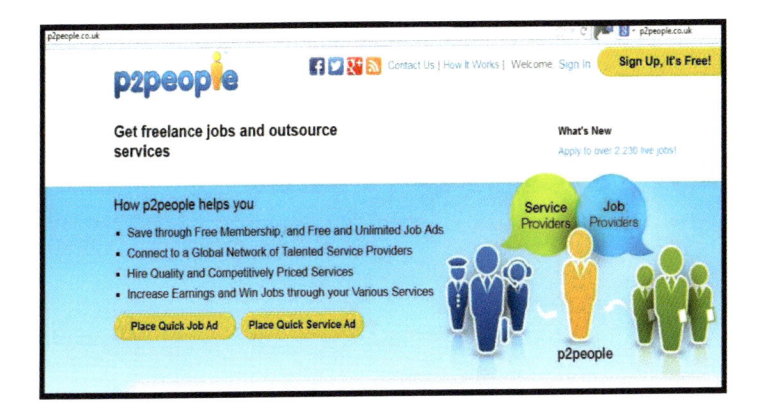

Contact Us | How It Works | Welcome Sign In

Sign Up, It's Free!

Get freelance jobs and outsource services

What's New
Apply to over 2,230 live jobs!

How p2people helps you

- Save through Free Membership, and Free and Unlimited Job Ads
- Connect to a Global Network of Talented Service Providers
- Hire Quality and Competitively Priced Services
- Increase Earnings and Win Jobs through your Various Services

Place Quick Job Ad **Place Quick Service Ad**

Service Providers   Job Providers

p2people

Website Title	Website URL LINK
Rent a coder | Hire IT freelancers	rent-acoder.com

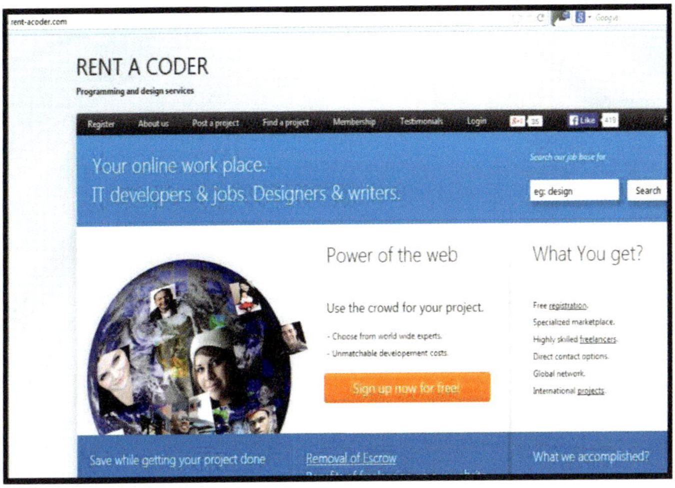
rent-acoder.com
RENT A CODER
Programming and design services
Register
About us
Post a project
Find a project
Membership
Testimonials
Login
Like
Your online work place.
IT developers & jobs. Designers & writers.
Search our job base for
eg: design
Search
Power of the web
Use the crowd for your project.
- Choose from world wide experts.
- Unmatchable developement costs.
Sign up now for free!
What You get?
Free registration.
Specialized marketplace.
Highly skilled freelancers.
Direct contact options.
Global network.
International projects.
Save while getting your project done
Removal of Escrow
What we accomplished?

Website Title	Website URL LINK
Codeur | a marketplace for IT freelancers	codeur.com

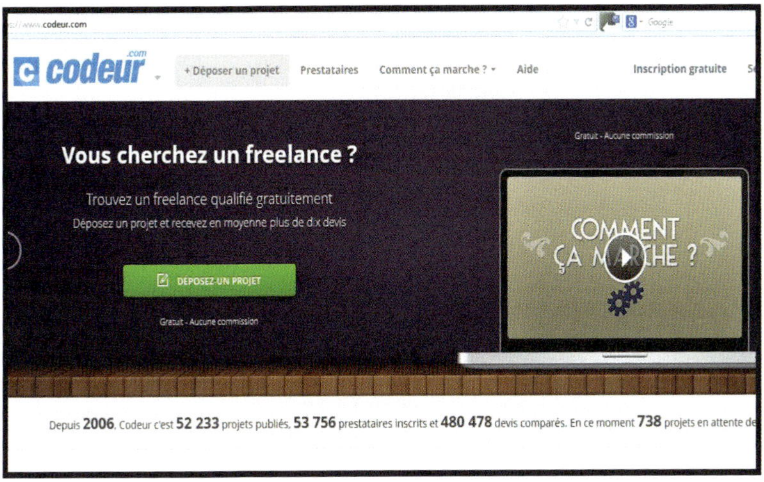
www.codeur.com
codeur .com
+ Déposer un projet
Prestataires
Comment ça marche ?
Aide
Inscription gratuite
Vous cherchez un freelance ?
Trouvez un freelance qualifié gratuitement
Déposez un projet et recevez en moyenne plus de dix devis
DÉPOSEZ UN PROJET
Gratuit - Aucune commission
Gratuit - Aucune commission
COMMENT ÇA MARCHE ?
Depuis 2006, Codeur c'est 52 233 projets publiés, 53 756 prestataires inscrits et 480 478 devis comparés. En ce moment 738 projets en attente de

Website Title	Website URL LINK
Guru | an online service marketplace connecting businesses with quality freelancers to get the job done	**guru.com**

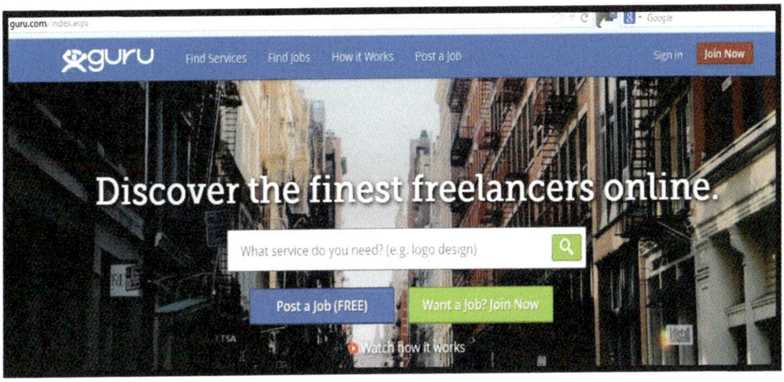
guru.com/index.aspx
guru
Find Services
Find Jobs
How it Works
Post a Job
Sign in
Join Now
Discover the finest freelancers online.
What service do you need? (e.g. logo design)
Post a Job (FREE)
Want a Job? Join Now
Watch how it works

Website Title	Website URL LINK
TaskArmy | connects clients with freelancers	taskarmy.com

task army

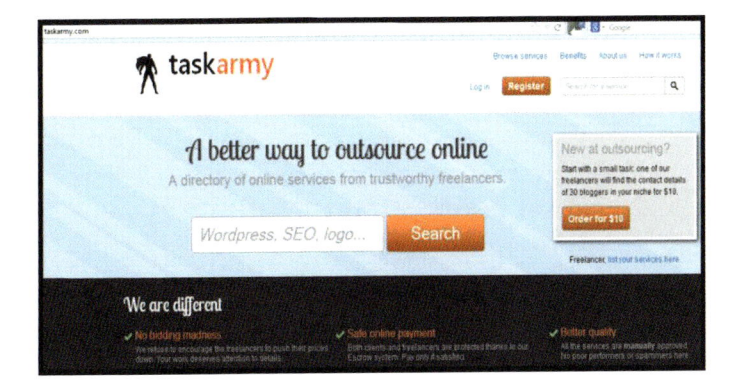

A better way to outsource online

A directory of online services from trustworthy freelancers.

New at outsourcing? Start with a small task: one of our freelancers will find the contact details of 30 bloggers in your niche for $10.

Order for $10

Freelancer, list your services here.

We are different

- **No bidding madness** — We refuse to encourage the freelancers to push their prices down. Your work deserves attention to details.
- **Safe online payment** — Both clients and freelancers are protected thanks to our Escrow system. Pay only if satisfied.
- **Better quality** — All the services are manually approved. No poor performers or spammers here.

Website Title	Website URL LINK
Projektbroker | an online portal connecting companies and individuals seeking to outsource jobs to freelancers from Central and Eastern Europe.	projektbroker.com

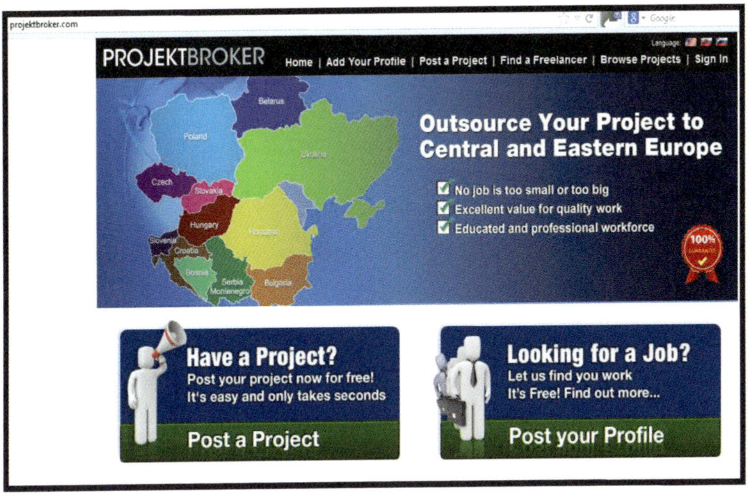
projektbroker.com
PROJEKTBROKER
Home | Add Your Profile | Post a Project | Find a Freelancer | Browse Projects | Sign In
Outsource Your Project to Central and Eastern Europe
No job is too small or too big
Excellent value for quality work
Educated and professional workforce
Have a Project?
Post your project now for free!
It's easy and only takes seconds
Post a Project
Looking for a Job?
Let us find you work
It's Free! Find out more...
Post your Profile

Website Title	Website URL LINK
Odesk | an employment platform enabling employers to hire, manage and pay a flexible online workforce and freelancers	odesk.com

Take a spin through our top freelancers

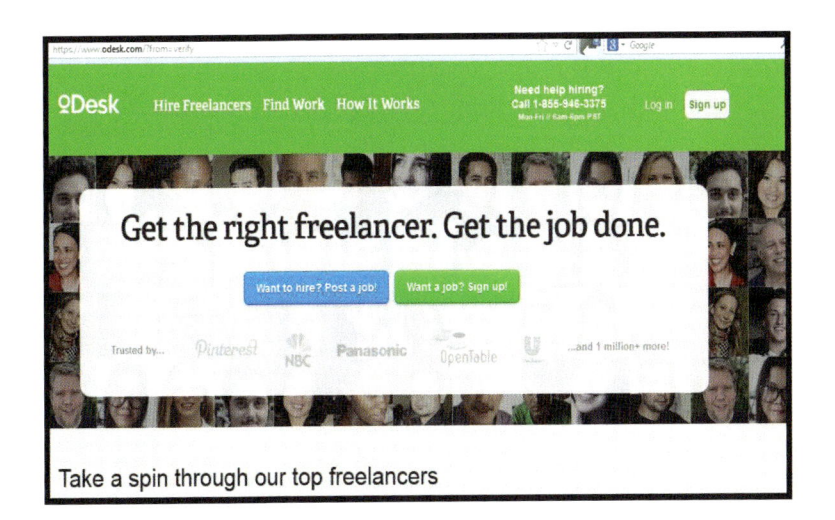

Website Title	Website URL LINK
idirect | marketplace for IT freelancers	idirect.fr

idirect.fr
NUMERO 1 DE L'HEBERGEMENT EN FRANCE
OVH.COM
Ici prochainement...
SITE EN CONSTRUCTION
Site hébergé par OVH.COM
Besoin d'assistance ?
1. Consultez nos guides :
Installer un module clef en main
Les outils à votre disposition :
Votre manager (espace client)
Net2Ftp

Website Title	Website URL LINK
ProgOnline | marketplace for IT freelancers	progonline.com

www.progonline.com
ProgOnline est également présent dans votre pays : United States
Inscrivez vous vite, gratuitement et sans engagement !
Liquidation.com
WHOLESALE AUCTIONS
BID NOW
PROG online
Plateforme N°1
pour vos projets informatiques
Identifiant
Identifiant
Mot de passe
OK
Inscription gratuite
Mot de passe perdu?
Accueil
Nouveau projet
Donneurs d'ordres
Développeurs
Blog
Témoignages
Rechercher [?]
Chercher
Vous recherchez un développeur ?
1. Publiez
Publiez gratuitement votre projet
2. Consultez
Consultez plusieurs offres de prestataires
3. Réalisez
Réalisez votre projet en sécurité
Je publie mon projet
Go
Développeurs, inscrivez-vous
Une question ?
Témoignages de nos clients
"J'étais sceptique au départ mais maintenant c'est en toute confiance que je renouvellerai des projets sur la plateforme."
"Le prestataire que nous avons choisi a été de bonne utilité et nous sommes content de la prestation. Réactif et ouvert. C'est ce que j'attendais."
"Très bons conseils, ça a été rapide et sans douleur pour le néophyte

Website Title	Website URL LINK
Reudes Missions | Hire, recruit your freelancers and find your next mission	ruedesmissions.com

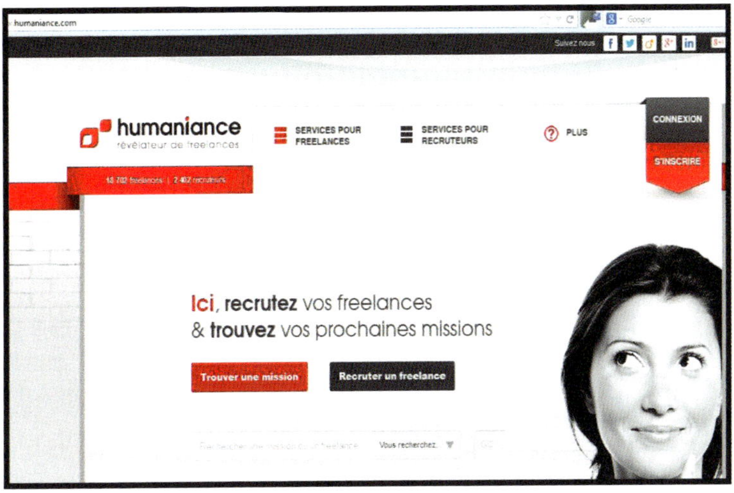

humaniance.com
Suivez nous
humaniance
révélateur de freelances
SERVICES POUR FREELANCES
SERVICES POUR RECRUTEURS
PLUS
CONNEXION
S'INSCRIRE
Ici, recrutez vos freelances
& trouvez vos prochaines missions
Trouver une mission
Recruter un freelance
Vous recherchez

Website Title	Website URL LINK
Prestataires | Find the best provider for your IT, Internet, Multimedia and IT projects	prestataires.com

prestataires.com
Annuaire prestataires
Espace prestataires
Prestataires.com
N°1 français de la recherche de prestataires NTIC, Internet, Multimédia et Informatiques
ACCUEIL
TROUVER UN PRESTATAIRE
COMMENT ÇA MARCHE ?
QUI SOMMES-NOUS ?
QUI SONT NOS PRESTATAIRES ?
NOS DOSSIERS
Trouvez
les meilleurs prestataires
pour vos projets NTIC, Internet, Multimédia et Informatiques
Quel est votre besoin ?
Création ou refonte de site Internet
Valider
RECEVEZ 3 À 5 DEVIS
de professionnels qualifiés
Gratuitement et sous 48H
Comment ça marche ?
Qui sommes-nous ?
Ils nous font confiance

Website Title	Website URL LINK
123 Presta | Provides clients with freelancers who can give them quotations on their projects	123presta.com

123presta.com
Google
123PRESTA
Vos devis Internet et informatique gratuits
8799
Prestataires Internet
2736 inscrits le mois dernier
BESOIN DE CONSEILS
BESOIN DE DEVIS
VOUS ÊTES PRESTATAIRES
CONTACT
123PRESTA
ESPACE PRIVÉ
123PRESTA.COM Devis gratuits pour vos projets internet et informatique + 8000 prestataires
A la recherche
de prestataires qualifiés ?
Site Internet
Référencement
Application mobile
123PRESTA
Comparateur de devis
BESOINS DE CONSEILS ?
Gratuit : Guides et modèles de cahier des charges
(Téléchargez vos modèles de cahier des charges, cahier des charges ecommerce, cahier des charges référencement...)
BESOIN DE 5 DEVIS MAX ?
GRATUIT
Recherche express (2min Max.)
(Nom du projet, fichier, raison sociale, téléphone, mail, délais ...)
123PRESTA.COM :
Avec plus de 5000 prestataires Internet et informatique, comparez plusieurs devis pour vos projets de site Internet, charte graphique, application mobile, logiciel informatique, maintenance informatique, le tout gratuitement.

Website Title	Website URL LINK
Companeo | Provides clients with freelancers who can give them quotations on their projects	companeo.com

companeo.com
COMPANEO
Trouver les bons fournisseurs, ça change tout !
0826 16 15 14 *
Sécurité : Obtenez plusieurs devis de spécialistes en vidéosurveillance
En savoir plus
Remplissez un questionnaire pour définir vos besoins
Nous qualifions et transmettons aux Fournisseurs Agréés
Vous recevez leurs devis sous 48h

Website Title	Website URL LINK
Quotatis | Provides clients with freelancers who can give them quotations on their projects	quotatis.fr

quotatis.fr
quotatis
1er réseau d'artisans depuis 1999
Comparez jusqu'à
5 devis travaux gratuits
d'artisans Quotatis disponibles dans votre région
DEVIS PAR TÉLÉPHONE
01 83 77 71 29
Vous êtes un pro ? 01 72 98 03 03
Economies d'énergies
Chauffage Climatisation
Portes - Fenêtres Vérandas
Cuisine Salle de bains
Peinture - Sol Revêtement
Jardin Piscine Terrasse
Electricité Alarme
Construction Rénovation
Toitures Façades
Traitements Petits travaux
JUSQU'À 30 000 EUROS À TAUX ZÉRO !
L'Etat vous propose un prêt à taux zéro pour réaliser vos travaux. La valeur du prêt accordé dépend des types et du nombre de travaux à réaliser.
Pour un bouquet deux travaux, la valeur du prêt est de 20.000 euros.
À partir de trois travaux, le prêt accordé est de 30.000 euros !
Je veux en profiter
0%
DEMANDEZ VOTRE DEVIS TRAVAUX EN 2 MINUTES
Mon projet : Cuisine, plombier, isolation
1 DÉCRIVEZ VOTRE PROJET EN 2MN
2 COMMUNIQUEZ VOS COORDONNÉES DÉTAILLÉES
3 RECEVEZ UNE LISTE DE 5 PROS
4 COMPAREZ DES DEVIS GRATUITS PERSONNALISÉS

Website Title	Website URL LINK
Easy Outsource | EasyOutsource is a place where Filipino online job seekers and international employers can connect. Becoming a member is 100% free.	easyoutsource.com

easyoutsource.com
easyoutsource
Log In
Sign Up
Home
Hire Workers
Get an Online Job
Get Started
Sign Up Free
Filipino Workers
Celeste May S. Tijamo
active 27 seconds ago
Ann Añover
active 30 seconds ago
Outsource work to the Philippines
EasyOutsource is a place where Filipino online job seekers and international employers can connect. Becoming a member is 100% free.
Find Great Workers – Talk to real people, hire the best.
Filipinos – Get an online job.
Reap the Benefits – Get more done, make more money.
Online Jobs
Software Developer
posted 32 minutes ago
Activation Emails
posted about 3 hours ago

Website Title	Website URL LINK
CloudCrowd | We bring together companies that need work done with people who want to work and get paid	cloudcrowd.com

cloudcrowd.com
CloudCrowd
We're working on it. Lots of us.
GET STARTED!
Home
How It Works
Worker Communities
Worker Resources
Support
Search here...
Go!
Work where and when you want.
Whether you're a stay-at-home parent, or a college student with an extra hour between classes, at CloudCrowd, you work on your schedule. Join today, and start turning your idle time into income.
Work on interesting and well paying tasks.
PROJECT NAME
TODAY'S RATE
Edit Documents.
Proofread and edit English writing.
$ 2.00
Review Documents.
$ 1.00

Website Title	Website URL LINK
CrowdFlower | Our technology then aggregates the results and controls for quality	crowdflower.com

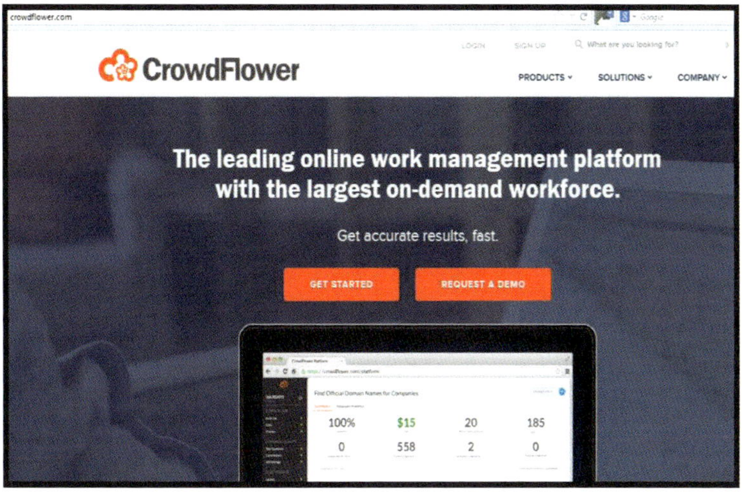
crowdflower.com
LOGIN
SIGN UP
What are you looking for?
CrowdFlower
PRODUCTS
SOLUTIONS
COMPANY
The leading online work management platform
with the largest on-demand workforce.
Get accurate results, fast.
GET STARTED
REQUEST A DEMO
100%
$15
20
185
0
558
2
0

Website Title	Website URL LINK
12designer | a CrowdSourcing web site dedicated to design projects, clients submit their missions, designers submit proposals, best design wins	12designer.com

12designer

| New project | Browse projects | Creatives |

+49 30 609895966
Weekdays 10 am - 6 pm CET

Design contests

Compare lots of different design ideas and walk away with the best one

Choose from a growing team of high quality and experienced creatives

The creative marketplace where logo, flyer and web design ideas are born!

16900+ clients have used—and loved—our service

29900+ experienced creatives are ready to offer solutions

100% money-back guarantee

Start a project ›

Featured in

ZEIT ONLINE | t3n | PAGE | WV | CREATION | 20 minuten | WELT ONLINE | crowdsourcing.org

Website Title	Website URL LINK
**99design	a CrowdSourcing web site dedicated to design projects**	99designs.com

99designs.com
Questions? Call us 1 800 513 1678
REQUEST A DESIGN CONSULTATI
designs
BROWSE CATEGORIES
HOW IT WORKS
PRICING
TESTIMONIALS
Get a design you'll love — guaranteed
Let our community of 283,022 designers create dozens of designs for you

Website Title	Website URL LINK
Blur Group | Crowdsource Creative marketing campaigns, design projects, content, artwork and innovation	blurgroup.com

| blurgroup.com | C | Google |

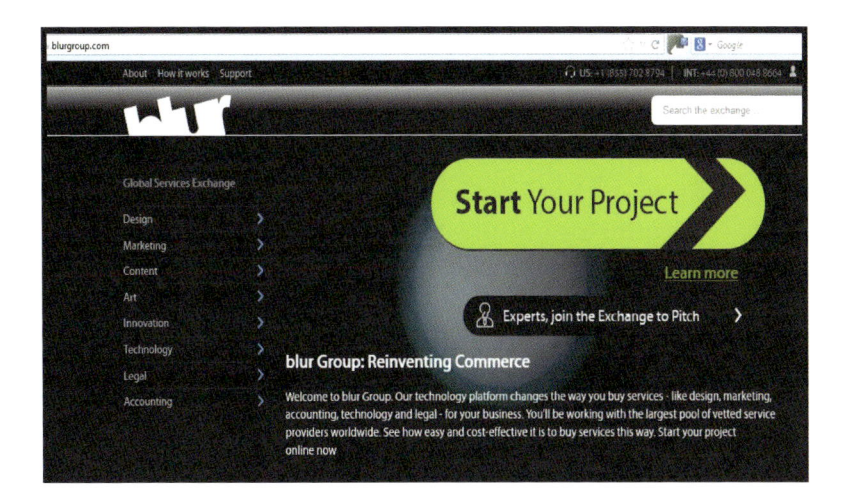

About | How it works | Support

US: +1 (855) 702 8734 | INT: +44 (0) 800 048 8664

Search the exchange

Global Services Exchange

- Design >
- Marketing >
- Content >
- Art >
- Innovation >
- Technology >
- Legal >
- Accounting >

Start Your Project >>

Learn more

Experts, join the Exchange to Pitch >

blur Group: Reinventing Commerce

Welcome to blur Group. Our technology platform changes the way you buy services - like design, marketing, accounting, technology and legal - for your business. You'll be working with the largest pool of vetted service providers worldwide. See how easy and cost-effective it is to buy services this way. Start your project online now

Website Title	Website URL LINK
Wexty | social network of mutual aid between private individuals	wexty.com

Choisissez votre interface préférée

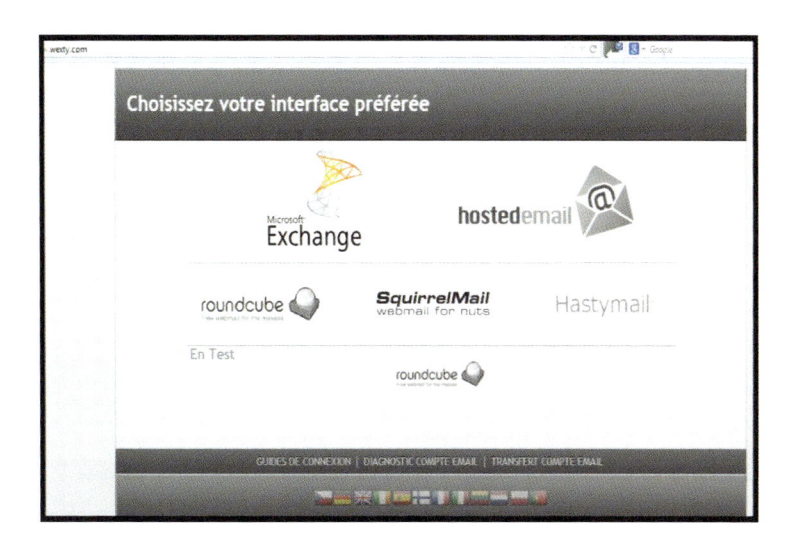

Microsoft Exchange

hostedemail

roundcube

SquirrelMail
webmail for nuts

Hastymail

En Test

roundcube

GUIDES DE CONNEXION | DIAGNOSTIC COMPTE EMAIL | TRANSFERT COMPTE EMAIL

Website Title	**Website URL LINK**
Catchafire | connects professionals who want to volunteer their skills with non-profits and social enterprises that need their help	catchafire.org

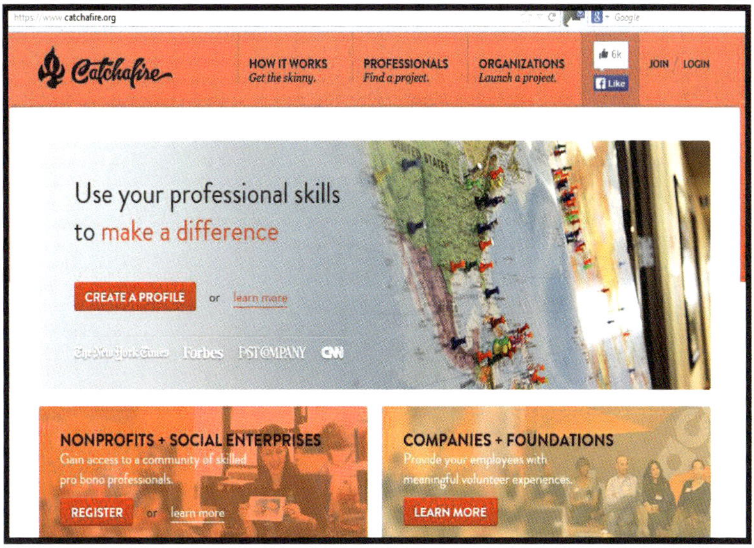
https://www.catchafire.org
Catchafire
HOW IT WORKS
Get the skinny.
PROFESSIONALS
Find a project.
ORGANIZATIONS
Launch a project.
6k
Like
JOIN / LOGIN
Use your professional skills
to make a difference
CREATE A PROFILE
or learn more
The New York Times Forbes FAST COMPANY CNN
NONPROFITS + SOCIAL ENTERPRISES
Gain access to a community of skilled pro bono professionals.
REGISTER
or learn more
COMPANIES + FOUNDATIONS
Provide your employees with meaningful volunteer experiences.
LEARN MORE

Website Title	Website URL LINK
IdeaConnection | gateway to a global network of experts, working in teams, led by world class facilitators	ideaconnection.com

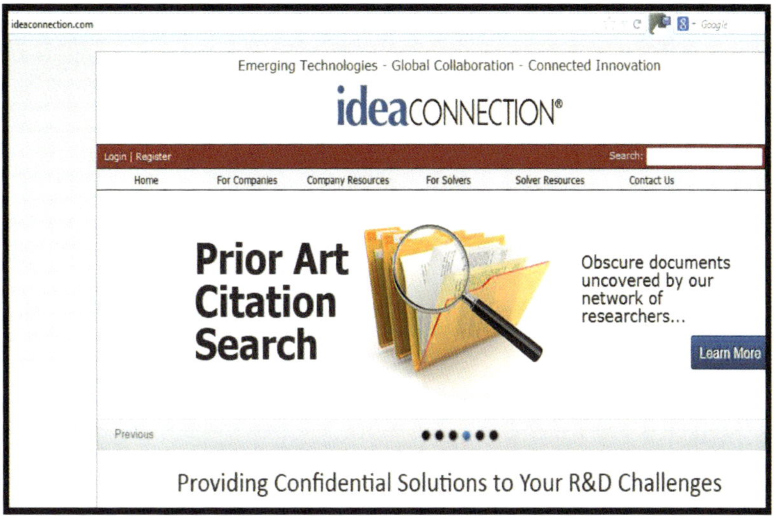
ideaconnection.com
Emerging Technologies - Global Collaboration - Connected Innovation
ideaCONNECTION®
Login | Register
Search:
Home
For Companies
Company Resources
For Solvers
Solver Resources
Contact Us
Prior Art Citation Search
Obscure documents uncovered by our network of researchers...
Learn More
Previous
Providing Confidential Solutions to Your R&D Challenges

Appendix: Stress and Anxiety Reducer Healthy Food and Recipes

Stress (Anxiety) Reducing Herbs, Food and Aromatherapy Oils.

Many of these herbs and spices are also known to help lower blood pressure.

Try these healing spices and herbs to flavor your foods

- Cayenne pepper (cayenne pepper is a powerful vasodilator, and may help expand blood vessels and ultimately help improve blood flow)

- Coconut water (full of nutrients, specially potassium, may help lower blood pressure levels)

- Raw Cacao (flavonoids and other anti-inflammatory nutrients in raw cacao may help deal the stress which is one of big cause of blood pressure problem)

- Turmeric (curcumin).(super food turmeric might help fight inflammation in the whole body, ultimately helping improve cardiovascular function and maintenance of healthy blood flow.)

- Basil (It might help lower your blood pressure)

- Ginger root: (might help fight inflammation in the whole body, ultimately helping improve cardiovascular function and maintenance of healthy blood flow)

- Lavender: (Lavender's leaves can be used in the same as you use rosemary. This relaxation herb may help lower your blood pressure)

- Cardamom (anti-oxidant, anti-inflammatory)

- Celery Seeds (anti-oxidant, anti-inflammatory)

- Hawthorn: (Hawthorn had been used in China for centuries to help lower high blood pressure)

- Red Hot Chili Pepper (Hot Chili peppers contain capsaicin that is known to increase metabolism and can help in weight loss. The weight loss can ultimately help lower blood pressure)

- Nutmeg: (Contains anti-inflammatory compounds, and may also help you stay calm by helping regulating mood swings, ultimately lower blood pressure)

- Rosemary: (Rosemary's anti- inflammation properties may help lower blood pressure)

- Cloves: (Good anti-inflammatory)

- Capers: (Antioxidants, vitamins, analgesic, anti-inflammatory)

- Black Pepper: (Good anti-inflammatory)

- Cayenne Pepper: (concentrated with minerals, vitamins and certain phytochemicals/nutrients, popular for anti-diabetic properties)

- Carom Seeds (Ajwain) (ajowan seeds are rich in fiber, minerals, vitamins, and anti-oxidants)

- Coriander Seeds (full of anti-oxidants, and excellent source of minerals like iron, copper, calcium, potassium, manganese, zincand magnesium)

- Fennel Seed: (contains numerous flavonoid anti-oxidants like kaempferol and quercetin. act as powerful anti-oxidants by removing harmful free radicals)

- Horseradish: (dietary fiber, vitamins, minerals, anti-oxidants, diuretic, have nerve soothing effects, anti-inflammatory)

- Mustard Seeds: (rich in phyto-nutrients, minerals, vitamins and anti-oxidants, regulating body metabolism)

- Tamarind: (certain health benefiting essential volatile chemical compounds, minerals, vitamins and dietary fiber.)

- Onion: (Antiseptic, may helps reduce high blood pressure, alleviates symptoms of asthma and colds)

- Sichuan Peppercorns: (source of vitamins such as vitamin A, carotenes, pyridoxine, and thiamin and minerals - manganese, potassium , copper, iron, phosphorous, selenium and zinc.)

- Lemon Peel: (Good source of minerals and vitamin C, a good cleaning agent, Alleviates congestion)

- Orange Peel: Good source of minerals and vitamin C, a good cleaning agent, Alleviates congestion)

- Peppermint: (anti-inflammatory, antioxidant, digestive aide)
  - Avocado
  - Bananas
  - Green Tea
  - Swiss Chard
  - Fatty Fish
  - Carrots
  - Milk
  - Yogurt
  - Nuts
  - Chocolate
  - Passionflower (Very calming and soothing)
  - Fennel seeds (helps strengthen the digestive system, where emotional stress is most likely to center.)
  - Feverfew (helps the body deal with muscular tension, head and neck tension).
  - Hops flower promotes sleep (helps dealing with restlessness).
  - Chamomile flowers
  - Schizandra fruit

- Ashwagandha (Indian ginseng)
- Lemon Balm
- Holy Basil
- Siberian Ginseng
- Licorice Root
- Kava Kava
- St. John's Wort (Please check with your Doctor if safe for you to consume)
- Lavender

Few Recipes

Garlic Shrimp

Hot Level:
Ice Cold, Mild, Spicy, Flaming, Scorcher

Prep Time: 15 minutes
Cook Time: 6 minutes

What You'll Need:

- 3 cloves of minced garlic
- 1/3 cup olive oil
- ¼ cup tomato sauce
- 2 tablespoons red wine vinegar
- 2 tablespoons fresh basil
- 2 pounds of shrimp
- ¼ teaspoon cayenne pepper

What You'll Do:

1. Mix up the garlic and tomato sauce and vinegar and oil. Add in the basil, and pepper.
2. Put in the shrimp and stir. Put in the refrigerator for about 45 minutes.
3. Grill for about 3 minutes or so on each side, then eat.

Grilled Shrimp

What You'll Need:

- 3 cloves of minced garlic
- 1/3 cup olive oil
- ¼ cup tomato sauce
- 2 tablespoons red wine vinegar
- 2 tablespoons fresh basil
- 2 pounds of shrimp
- ¼ teaspoon cayenne pepper

What You'll Do:

1. Mix up the garlic and tomato sauce and vinegar and oil. Add in the basil, and pepper.
2. Put in the shrimp and stir. Put in the refrigerator for about 45 minutes.
3. Grill for about 3 minutes or so on each side, then eat.

Curry Chicken

Ingredients:

4 PCS Chicken breast (boneless, skinless) (cut into bite size cubes)

1 medium (chopped) onion

4 minced garlic cloves

1 medium ginger rood (chopped)

1 Medium size tomatoes

1 small can of (UNSLATED) tomato sauce

2 tsp curry powder

1 tsp turmeric powder

2 tsp *Garam Masala* (from Indian Grocery Store or Trader Joe's)

½ tsp. cumin powder

1/4 tsp. hot chili powder

3 tbsp. olive oil

Sea salt and ground pepper to taste (less salt is better)

Procedure:

1. In a large skillet on medium-low heat, add olive oil, sauté chopped onions until soft (about 4 to 7 minutes). Add the chopped garlic, minced garlic, the all the spices and cook 2 minutes.
2. Add chopped tomatoes, and tomato sauce. Whisk thoroughly and begin to bring to a simmer.
3. Add the chicken pieces, cover for 15 minutes, or until chicken is done.
4. Enjoy hot and fresh!
5. You can also try with brown rice or quinoa.

Makes 4 Servings

Ginger-Garlic Mahi-Mahi Fillets

What you need:

4 Mahi - Mahi fillets (8 oz)
1 Cup low fat yogurt
4 tsp balsamic vinegar
1 tsp fresh lemon juice
2 tsp grated fresh ginger root
2 clove crushed garlic
6 tsp olive oil
Black pepper to taste

What You need to Do:

1. In a big bowl, mix yogurt, lemon juice, balsamic vinegar, ginger, garlic and half of the olive oil (3tbsp). Season fish filets with black pepper. Put the mahi-mahi fillets in this bowl (rub the fish with the mixture of this marinate).
2. Cover the marinated fish in the bowl and put in the refrigerator for 1/2 to 1 hour.
3. Heat the rest of the olive oil (3tbsp) in a large skillet over medium heat. Remove fish from the bowl, and reserve yogurt-marinade. Fry fish for about 5 minutes (each side). Pour rest of the yogurt-marinade over the fish in the pan and heat over medium heat for 2-3 minutes
4. Enjoy hot and fresh!
5. You can also try with brown rice or quinoa.

Makes 4 Servings

Nutty Mahi-Mahi

What You Need:

4 Mahi - Mahi fillets (8 oz)
4 eggs
4 cups Whole Wheat (unsalted) bread crumbs
½ cup Pine nuts
½ cup sliced (bleached) almonds
2 tsp fresh lemon juice
4 to 8 leaves fresh mint leaves
4 tsp olive oil

What You need to Do:

1. In a blender (food processor), blend the nuts (pine nuts and almonds), with bread crumbs, eggs, lemon juice, mint leaves and olive oil.
2. Marinate the fish with this blended marinate and refrigerate for 2 hours.
3. Pre heat the oven to 375 to 400 degree F and bake the fish for about 20 minutes (until cooked well).
4. Enjoy hot and fresh!
5. You can also try with brown rice or quinoa.

   Makes 4 Servings

Garlic Lemon Zest Mahi-Mahi Fillets

What you need:

4 Mahi - Mahi fillets (8 oz)

4 tsp balsamic vinegar

2 tsp fresh Lemon Juice

1/4 cup grapefruit juice

2 tsp grated fresh Lemon Zest

1tsp Lemon salt

2 clove crushed garlic

6 tsp olive oil

What You need to Do:

1. In a big bowl, mix all the ingredients to make the marinate.
2. Put the mahi-mahi fillets in this bowl (rub the fish with the mixture of this marinate).
3. Cover the marinated fish in the bowl and put in the refrigerator for 3 to 4 hour.
6. Pre heat the oven to 375 to 400 degree F and bake the fish for about 20 minutes (until cooked well).
7. Enjoy hot and fresh!
4. You can also try with brown rice or quinoa.

Makes 4 Servings

Grilled Ginger Chicken

Ingredients:

1 cup Orange juice

1 medium size piece of fresh ground ginger root

6 tsp olive oil

2 Freshly crushed garlic cloves

4 PCS Chicken breast (boneless, skinless)

Procedure:

1. Mix all the ingredients to make the marinate.
2. Marinate the chicken breast pieces and refrigerate for 2 hours.
8. Pre heat the oven to 400 degree F and bake the chicken pieces for about 25 to 30 minutes (until cooked well).
9. Enjoy hot and fresh!
5. You can also try with brown rice or quinoa.

   Makes 4 Servings

Grilled Basil-Thyme-Ginger Chicken

Ingredients:

3 tsp. fresh Thyme, chopped

3 tsp. fresh Basil, chopped

1 cup Tomatoes with juice

1 medium size piece of fresh ground ginger root

6 tsp olive oil

4 PCS Chicken breast (boneless, skinless)

Procedure:

3. Mix all the ingredients to make the marinate.
4. Marinate the chicken breast pieces and refrigerate for 2 hours.
10. Pre heat the oven to 400 degree F and bake the chicken pieces for about 25 to 30 minutes (until cooked well).
11. Enjoy hot and fresh!
6. You can also try with brown rice or quinoa.

Makes 4 Servings

Perfect Hardboiled Egg

Hot Level:
Ice Cold, Mild, Spicy, Flaming, Scorcher

Prep Time: 5 minutes
Cook Time: 20 minutes

What You'll Need:

- 6 cups of water
- 8 eggs

What You'll Do:

1. Mix together the water and vinegar in a big pot.
2. Add the eggs before the water begins to boil.
3. Bring it to a boil on high.
4. Reduce the heat to a low setting and cook for 14 minutes or so.
5. Remove and cool. Enjoy plain or with any other entrée or side.

Main Dish: *The Perfect Hardboiled Egg*

What You'll Need:

- 1 tablespoon of salt
- 6 cups of water
- 8 eggs
- ¼ cup distilled white vinegar

What You'll Do:

1. Mix together the salt and water and vinegar in a big pot.
2. Add the eggs before the water begins to boil.
3. Bring it to a boil on high.
4. Reduce the heat to a low setting and cook for 14 minutes or so.
5. Remove and cool. Enjoy plain or with any other entrée or side.

Sides

Baked Kale Chips

What You'll Need:
- 1 bunch of kale
- 1 tablespoon olive oil

What You'll Do:

6. Preheat oven to 350 degrees F and line a non-insulated cookie sheet with parchment paper.
7. Remove the leaves from the stems and tear them into bite-sized pieces. Wash them carefully and dry.
8. Drizzle olive oil over top the kale.
9. Bake until the edges are brown, about 10-15 minutes.

Sugar Snap Peas

What You'll Need:

- ½ pound sugar snap peas
- 1 tablespoon olive oil
- 1 tablespoon chopped shallots
- 1 teaspoon chopped thyme
- Kosher salt to taste *(less or no salt will be better)*

What You'll Do:

1. Preheat oven to 450 degrees F.
2. Spread the peas onto a baking sheet.
3. Brush them with the olive oil.
4. Add on the shallots, thyme, and salt on top of the peas.
5. Bake the peas for 6 to 10 minutes (until firm but not burnt).
6. Cool and enjoy.

Sides:

Sugar Snap Peas

What You'll Need:

- ½ pound sugar snap peas
- 1 tablespoon olive oil
- 1 tablespoon chopped shallots
- 1 teaspoon chopped thyme
- Kosher salt to taste (**NO SALT IS BETTER**!)

What You'll Do:

1. Preheat oven to 450 degrees F.
2. Spread the peas onto a baking sheet.
3. Brush them with the olive oil.
4. Add on the shallots, thyme, and salt on top of the peas.
5. Bake the peas for 6 to 10 minutes (until firm but not burnt).

Cool and enjoy.

Mojito Punch

What You'll Need:

- ½ cup lime juice
- ½ cup fresh mint leaves
- *-1/2 stevia (sweetner)*
- 4 ¼ cups   soda
- 4 cups crushed ice

What You'll Do:

1. Combine the lime juice, mint leaves, and sweetener together in a bowl or pitcher.
2. Take the mint leaves and lightly bruise them with a spoon.
3. Pour the   soda into the juice mixture and add the sweetener.
4. Mix in the crushed ice and serve cold.

Spiced Applesauce

What You'll Need:

- 15 apples, peeled, cored, diced
- 1 teaspoon ground cinnamon
- 1 cup water
- 1/2 teaspoon grated nutmeg
- 1 tablespoon lemon juice
- 1/2 teaspoon ground allspice
- -1/2 *stevia (sweetner)*
- 1/2 teaspoon ground black pepper

What You'll Do:

1. Mix apples, water, lemon juice, and *stevia* in a pot on medium heat. Add cinnamon, nutmeg, allspice, and pepper.
2. Simmer the mixture while stirring and cook for around 15 minutes.
3. Mash the apples until preferable consistency.
4. Remove the pot and cool the applesauce in the refrigerator. Take out and serve cold.

Smoothie

What You'll Need:

- ½ cup plain Greek yogurt
- ¼ cup frozen blueberries
- 1/3 cup unsweetened almond milk
- 1 cup loosely packed spinach
- 1 scoop vanilla protein powder
- 1/3 cup ice

What You'll Do:

1. Add ingredients, two at a time, and blend until smooth and creamy.
2. Add ice last and serve cold.

Tabbouleh

This Mediterranean favorite is so good for you, but you can make it even healthier. Using concepts and acceptable ingredients on the Dash Diet you can forever change this into an even better alternative. Eat it on its own as a side dish or appetizer or enjoy it as a salad for lunch or dinner. You will love the burst of flavors!

Serves 8

Ingredients

1 1/2 cups water
3/4 cup bulgur (cracked wheat), rinsed and drained
1 cup diced, seeded tomatoes
1 cup chopped parsley
1/2 cup chopped scallions or green onions
1 teaspoon dill weed
4 black olives, sliced
1/4 cup lemon juice
2 tablespoons extra-virgin olive oil
Freshly ground black pepper, to taste

Preparation:

In a small saucepan, bring the water to a boil. Remove from heat and add the bulgur. Cover and let stand until the bulgur is tender and the liquid is completely absorbed, about 15 to 20 minutes.

In a large bowl, add the bulgur and the remaining ingredients. Toss gently just until the ingredients are evenly distributed. Cover and refrigerate for 2 hours to allow the flavors to blend. Serve chilled.

Mediterranean Chicken and Red Potatoes

A delicious blend of flavors that is inspired by classic Mediterranean ideas, and that means that you will love every bite. The potatoes are in the perfect amount and it shows that you can have a classic favorite without any of the guilt. So good that you may make this a regular part of the meal rotation and enjoy just how delicious healthy cooking can really be.

Ingredients:
1 1/2 lbs. boneless skinless chicken breasts, cut into 1-inch cubes
1 lb. Yukon Gold potatoes, cut into 3/4-inch cubes
1 medium onion, coarsely chopped
1/2 cup reduced-fat Greek or olive oil vinaigrette
1/4 cup lemon juice
1 tsp dry oregano
1 tsp minced garlic
1/2 cup chopped tomato

Preparation:
Mix all ingredients except tomatoes in a large bowl. Place equal amounts onto 4 large squares of heavy-duty foil. Fold in top and sides of each to enclose filling, leaving room for air to circulate.

Grill over medium heat for about 25 to 30 minutes or until chicken is cooked through and red potatoes are soft. Carefully open packets and sprinkle equal amounts of tomato over each.

Note: Packets may also be baked at 400°F for 30 minutes instead of grilling.

Mediterranean Bean Dip

This is one of those snacks that you could just live on! You will love the flavors all coming together and enjoy this unique twist on a classic bean dip. Rather than purchasing an already made bean dip that is full of fat and sodium, this makes for a great twist that is right in line with eating on the Dash Diet.

Ingredients:
2 15-ounce cans, rinsed and drained, or 3 1/2 cups cooked garbanzo or navy beans
2/3 cup fat-free sour cream
2 tsp minced garlic
4 tbsp balsamic vinegar
1/4 cup chopped sun-dried tomatoes (not in oil)
1/4 cup finely chopped fresh or dried parsley
2 tbsp chopped Kalamata or ripe olives
Kalamata olives, as garnish
Assorted vegetables and crackers for serving

Preparation:
In the bowl of a food processor blend the beans, sour cream, garlic, and vinegar until smooth; stir in sundried tomatoes, parsley, and chopped olives.
Place the mix in a serving bowl and garnish with olives. Serve with assorted vegetables and crackers for dipping.
Dip can be made ahead of time and refrigerated overnight or for 2 to 3 hours to allow flavors to blend.

Roasted Garlic

What You'll Need:

- One head of garlic, medium sized
- 2 tablespoons of olive oil

What You'll Do:

1. Preheat the oven to 250 degrees F.
2. Cut the top off the clove of garlic and put into a dish for baking.
3. Add olive oil on top and bake for 20 minutes.
4. Cool and then use hands to squeeze out the soft garlic.

Sides:

Roasted Garlic

What You'll Need:

- One head of garlic, medium sized
- 2 tablespoons of olive oil

What You'll Do:

1. Preheat the oven to 250 degrees F.
2. Cut the top off the clove of garlic and put into a dish for baking.
3. Add olive oil on top and bake for 20 minutes.
4. Cool and then use hands to squeeze out the soft garlic.

Fruity Fruit Juice

What You'll Need:

- 1 Granny Smith apple
- 1 pear
- 1 pitted peach

What You'll Do:

1. Yet another simple, yet delicious recipe. All you have to do is juice and serve.
2. Best chilled.

Fruity Fruit Juice

What You'll Need:

- 1 Granny Smith apple
- 1 pear
- 1 pitted peach

What You'll Do:

6. Yet another simple, yet delicious recipe. All you have to do is juice and serve.

Best chilled

What You'll Need:

- 1 beet
- 4 carrots
- 1 cucumber
- 3 celery stalks

What You'll Do:

1. Probably the simplest recipe out there—juice and serve.
2. Tastes great chilled or warm.

Veggie Juice

Veggie Juice

What You'll Need:
- 1 beet
- 4 carrots
- 1 cucumber
- 3 celery stalks

What You'll Do:
10. Probably the simplest recipe out there—juice and serve.
11. Tastes great chilled or warm.

Triplesec

What You'll Need:
- 1 tomato
- 4 celery stalks
- 4 carrots

What You'll Do:
1. Juice and serve right away.
2. For a twist on this delicious drink, add a couple of your favorite spices and serve warm.

Drinks *Triple sec*

What You'll Need:
- 1 tomato
- 4 celery stalks
- 4 carrots

What You'll Do:

12. Juice and serve right away.
13. For a twist on this delicious drink, add a couple of your favorite spices and serve warm.

Crunchy Edamame

What You'll Need:

- 1 (12 ounce) package edamame or green soybeans (frozen and without shells)
- *1/2 spoon black peppers*
- 1 tablespoon olive oil

What You'll Do:

1. Preheat oven to 400 degrees F.
2. Rinse and thaw the edamame under water and drain
3. Place the beans onto a baking pan or dish and then add olive oil over top of them.
4. *black peppers*
5. Bake for about 10 to 15 minutes until the crunchy.

REFERENCES

1. Adams, G. A. & Jex, S. M. (1997). Confirmatory factor analysis of the time management behaviour scale. *Psychological Reports, 80*, 225-226.
2. Manage Your Day-to-Day: Build Your Routine, Find Your Focus, and Sharpen Your Creative Mind (The 99U Book Series) Paperback
3. by Jocelyn K. Glei
4. The DNA of Success: Know What You Want to Get What You Want, by Jack M. Zufelt
5. Barling, J., Kelloway, E. K. & Cheung, D. (1996). Time management and achievement striving interact to predict car sale performance. *Journal of Applied Psychology, 81*, 821-826.
6. Baruch, E., Bruno, J., Horn, L. (1987) Dimensions of time use attitudes among middle high SES students. Social Behaviour & Personality: An International Journal, 15, 1-12. Retrieved from **http://www.sbp-journal.com/**
7. Time Management: The Secrets Of Time Management, How To Beat Procrastination, Manage Your Daily Schedule & Be More Productive For Life (Time management, ... life, Business, Developmental psychology)
8. **Time Management: Increase Your Personal Productivity And Effectiveness (Harvard Business Essentials)** by Harvard Business School Press (Jun 1, 2005)
9. Bond, M. & Feather, N. (1988). Some correlates of structure and purpose in the use of time. *Journal of Personality and Social Psychology, 55*, 321-329.

10. Cemaloglu, N., & Filiz, S. (2010). The relation between time management skills and academic achievement of potential teachers. Educational Research Quarterly, 33, 3-23. Retrieved from **http://erquarterly.org/**

11. **Time Management In an Instant: 60 Ways to Make the Most of Your Day (In an Instant (Career Press))** by Karen Leland and Keith Bailey

12. Claessens, B. J. C., van Erde, W., Rutte, C. G. & Roe, R. A. (2005). A review of the time management literature. *Personnel Review, 36*, 255-276.

13. Craig, L. & Bittman, M. (2008). The incremental time costs of children: An analysis of children's impact on adult time use in Australia. *Feminist Economics, 14*, 59-88.

14. Green, L. V., Kolesar, P. J., & Ward, W. (2007). Coping with time-varying demand when setting staffing requirements for a service system. *Production and Operations Management, 16*, 13-39.

15. Duffin, C. (2009). Community nurses find an extra five hours. *Primary Health Care, 19*, 8-9.

16. Eldeleklioglu, J., Yilmaz, A., & Gultekin, F. (2010). **Investigation of teacher trainee's psychological well-being in terms of time management**. *Procedia Social and Behavioral Sciences, 2*, 342-348. doi:10.1016/j.sbspro.2010.03.022

17. **Time Management: Commit To Controlling Time** by **Michael Dunar** (May 31, 2013)

18. **Time Management 2.0: 15 Secrets of a Self-Made Millionaire for Getting Things Done (Coffee With A Millionaire)...** by Hank Reardon (Oct 2, 2013)

19. Esters, I. G. & Castellanos, E. F. (1998). *Time management behavior as a predictor of role-related stress: Implications for school counselors*.

20. Ferrar, K. E., Olds, T. S., & Walters, J. L. (2012). All the stereotypes confirmed: Differences in how Australian boys and girls use their time. *Health Education & Behavior, 39*, 589-595.

21. Ferrari, J., Özer, B.U., & Demir, A. (2009). Chronic procrastination among Turkish adults. *Journal of Social Psychology, 149*, 302-308.

22. Natural Healing College Authors (2013) Alternative Medicine Treatments: The **Holistic Health** Practitioner seeks to take care of the root causes of disease, rather than merely eliminating or suppressing the symptoms

23. Garcia-Ros, R., Perez-Gonzalez, F., & Hinojosa, E. (2004). The construction and evaluation of a time management scale with Spanish high school students. *School Psychology International, 25*(2), 167-183.

24. Hellsten, L. M. (2012). **What do we know about time management? A review of the literature and a psychometric critique of instruments assessing time management**. In T. Stoilov (Ed.), *Time Management* (pp. 3-28). Croatia: InTech.

25. Huang, E. Y. (2008). ***How personality affects time control over e-mail use: The mediating effects***.

26. Koch, C. J., & Kleinmann, M. (2002). A stitch in time saves nine: Behavioural decision-making explanations for time management problems. *European Journal of Work and Organisational Psychology, 11*(2), 199-217.

27. LeFebvre, K. B. (2009). Prioritize and take stock of you life. *ONS Connect, 24*, 20.

28. Macan, T. H. (1994). Time management: Test of a process model. *Journal of Applied Psychology, 79*(3), 381-391.

29. Macan, T. H. (1996). Time management training: Effects on time behaviours, attitudes, and job performance. *Journal of Psychology, 130*, 229-236.

30. Mudrack, P. E. (1997). The structure of perceptions of time. *Educational and Psychological Measurement, 57*, 222-240. doi: 10.1177/0013164497057002003

31. http://www.yogajournal.com

32. http://en.wikipedia.org

33. http://www.wikihow.com

34. http://en.wikipedia.org/wiki/Pranayama

35. http://en.wikipedia.org/wiki/Yoga

36. http://en.wikipedia.org/wiki/Stress

37. http://en.wikipedia.org/wiki/Stress_management

38. http://www.indiaparenting.com/alternative-healing/12_2659/kapalbhati-pranayama-a-breathing-exercise.html

39. http://www.yogameditation.com/Articles/Issues-of-Bindu/Bindu-13/Why-hold-your-breath

40. Nonis, S. A., Hudson, G. I., Logan, L. B. & Ford, C. W. (1998). Influence of perceived control over time on college students' stress and stress-related outcomes. *Research in Higher Education, 39*(5), 587-604.

41. Orlikowsky, W. J. & Yates, J. (2002). Its about time: Temporal structuring in organizations. *Organization Science, 13*, 684-700.

42. Seo, E. H. (2009). The relationship of procrastination with a mastery goal versus and avoidance goal. *Social Behaviour and Personality, 37*, 911-920.

43. Shanahi, C., Weiner, R. & Streit, M. K. (1993). An investigation of the dispositional nature of the time management construct. *Anxiety, Stress and Coping, 6,* 231-243.

44. Steel, P. (2007). The nature of procrastination: A meta-analytic and theoretical review of quintessential self-regulatory failure. *Psychological Bulletin, 133,* 65-94.

45. Tice, D., & Baumeister, R. (1997). Longitudinal study of procrastination, performance, stress, and health: The costs and benefits of dawdling. *Psychological Science, 8*(6), 454-458. doi:10.1111/j.1467-9280.1997.tb00460.x

46. Xiting, H., & Zhijie, Z. (2001). The compiling of adolescence time management disposition inventory. *Acta Psychologica Sinica, 33,* 338-343.

47. wikihow and wikipedia

Other Recommended Reads:

Shawn Chhabra
Best Selling Author

Books by Shawn Chhabra

ABOUT THE AUTHOR

Shawn Chhabra is a successful entrepreneur, educator, business coach and marketing executive who resides in Saint Louis, MO. He holds both his Bachelor's and Master's degree, and places great emphasis on a solid education. Shawn has leveraged his educational background to become an author, coach, mentor, and curriculum creator for several online institutions.

Shawn has worked within several industries including food, clothing, retail, IT, and holistic health. He is a big believer in healthy living, and has put this concept into play with his work directly. He is very in tune with practicing what he preaches, and often writes about his life experiences to enrich the lives of others.

A Man Who Wants To Reach Others Through His Passions

Shawn has always wanted to reach people through education. He brings his vast
expertise of business and holistic practices to his coaching and publishing business.
Shawn believes in treating his clients like they are his brothers and sisters—this is
modeled after his favorite Sanskrit saying: "the world is one family."
Shawn is featured as one of the America's PremierExperts® at

http://www.americaspremierexperts.com/directory/shawn-chhabra.php.

In the process of expanding educationally and professionally, Shawn mastered the
process of Defining-Refining (TM). This is a process utilizing the continuous evaluation
and tweaking of strategies in order to lower the risk of losses.

Shawn Has Put What He Has Learned Into Words For Others

Shawn Chhabra has authored several books, including the #1 Best Seller:
Weight Loss by Quitting Sugar and Carb (ISBN-10: 1494449285, B00GUXOCNM),
and *Dash Diet: Heart Health* (ISBN-10: 1494966212, B00HAVX3UQ)

Shawn is happily married to the beautiful Indu, and they have four wonderful children.
He understands the value of family and this is his first priority in life. Shawn and
Indu are proud parents of three daughters, Anshul, Taniya, Tarika and their son Anuj
(Sunny) and son-in-law Matt Schwartzkopf.

Shawn and Indu have co-managed their wholesale computer business for the last 14
years. The computer business website can be visited at: www.laptopuniverse.com.
Shawn has a website where he puts all of his work and practice into play and it is:

http://www.shawnchhabra.com

https://www.linkedin.com/in/shawnchhabrausa

where you can learn even more about him and his work.

Shawn has also been quoted in national media networks, such as ABC, CBS, NBC, CNN and Fox affiliates.

Shawn's favorite quote:
Give a man a fish and you feed him for a day.
Teach a man to fish and you feed him for a lifetime.
~ Traditional Proverb

America's PremierExperts

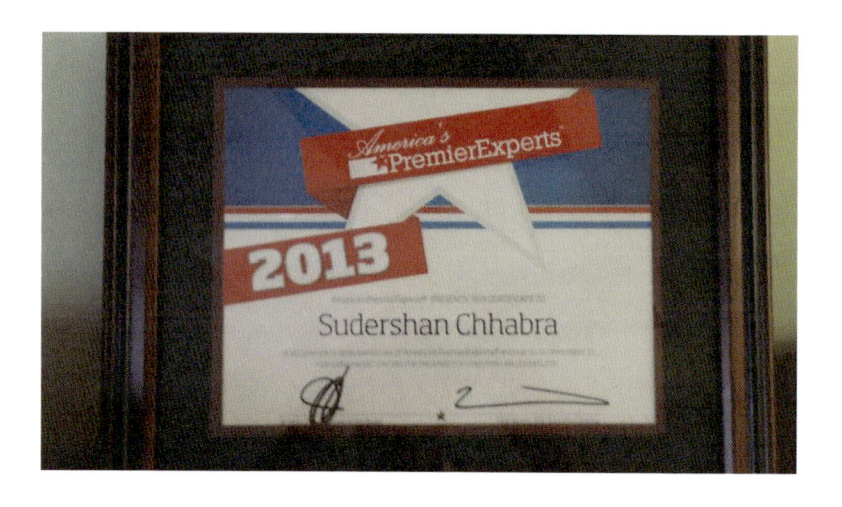

2013

Sudershan Chhabra

Weight Loss, Addiction and Detox
Weight Loss
Best Seller
amazon.com
Quitting
Sugar
and
Carb
Learn How to Overcome Sugar Addiction
A Sugar Buster Super Detox Diet
Shawn Chhabra
Milo E Newton
Healthy Life Naturally Publication
FREE RECIPE BOOK

DASH DIET

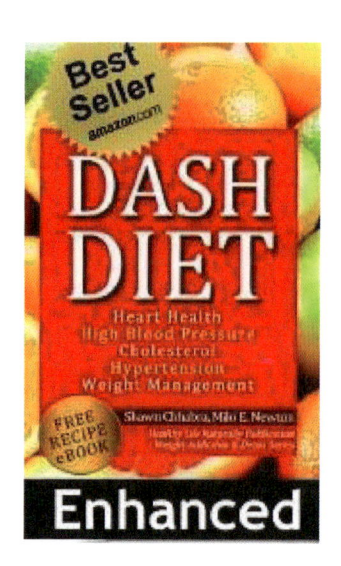

Best Seller amazon.com

Heart Health
High Blood Pressure
Cholesterol
Hypertension
Weight Management

Shawn Chhabra, Milo E. Newton

Healthy Life Naturally Publication
Weight Addiction & Detox Series

FREE RECIPE eBOOK

Enhanced

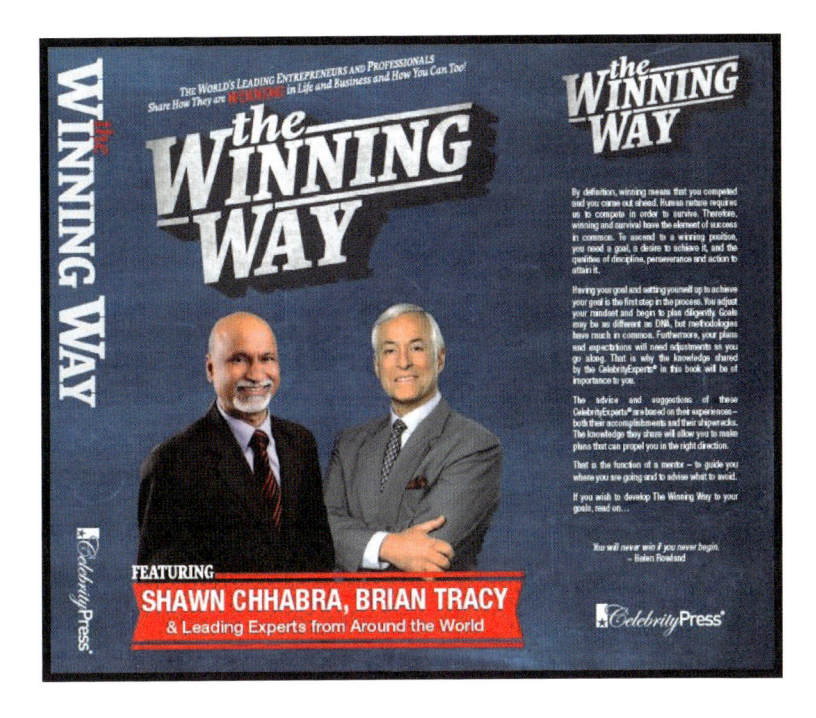

THE WORLD'S LEADING ENTREPRENEURS AND PROFESSIONALS
Share How They are WINNING in Life and Business and How You Can Too!

the WINNING WAY

the WINNING WAY

By definition, winning means that you competed and you came out ahead. Human nature requires us to compete in order to survive. Therefore, winning and survival have the element of success in common. To ascend to a winning position, you need a goal, a desire to achieve it, and the qualities of discipline, perseverance and action to attain it.

Having your goal and setting yourself up to achieve your goal is the first step in the process. You adjust your mindset and begin to plan diligently. Goals may be as different as DNA, but methodologies have much in common. Furthermore, your plans and expectations will need adjustments as you go along. That is why the knowledge shared by the CelebrityExperts® in this book will be of importance to you.

The advice and suggestions of these CelebrityExperts® are based on their experiences — both their accomplishments and their shipwrecks. The knowledge they share will allow you to make plans that can propel you in the right direction.

That is the function of a mentor — to guide you where you are going and to advise what to avoid.

If you wish to develop The Winning Way to your goals, read on...

You will never win if you never begin.
— Helen Rowland

FEATURING
SHAWN CHHABRA, BRIAN TRACY
& Leading Experts from Around the World

CelebrityPress®

LIFE STRESS TIME MANAGEMENT

Do you feel like you are not in control of your life? Do you struggle to figure out how to get everything done in a day? Are you worried that you can't stay organized or stay ahead of the game? If you want to take your life back and truly enjoy the time that you have, then this "Time Management" book is for you!

The "Time Management" is a book that shows you what it really means to stay in control of your life. Though you may feel bogged down by commitments and a lack of time to complete them all, sometimes it's simply a matter of staying organized. This book, written by Shawn Chhabra, can be an excellent tool in helping you to do just that.

It's Time To Take Control of Your Time and Your Life and Learn How To Do That

SHAWN CHHABRA

Sudershan Chhabra a.k.a. **Shawn Chhabra** is a successful entrepreneur, educator, business coach and marketing executive. He holds a Bachelor's and Master's degree, and places great emphasis on a solid education. Shawn is a best-selling award winning author and is featured as one of the America's PremierExpert ® at:

http://www.americanpremierexperts.com/shawn-chhabra.php

Shawn is the proud co-author of the forthcoming book **"THE WINNING WAY"** with Brian Tracy.

Shawn is happily married to his beautiful wife, Indu and they have four wonderful children. He understands the value of family and this is his first priority in life.

http://www.shawnchhabra.com

TIME MANAGEMENT

TIME MANAGEMENT

LIFE MANAGEMENT
STRESS MANAGEMENT
Ideas, Tools, Tips, Hints and Habits
Time Management Tools
Productivity Resources and Techniques
Healthy and Happy Lifestyle- Habits and Tips

From the co-author of forthcoming book
"THE WINNING WAY" WITH **BRIAN TRACY**

SHAWN CHHABRA